WHO AM I?

WHO AM I?

by

NORMAN P. GRUBB

CHRISTIAN LITERATURE CRUSADE
Fort Washington, Pennsylvania 19034

CHRISTIAN LITERATURE CRUSADE
Fort Washington, Pennsylvania 19034

First published 1974
Second Impression 1975
Third Impression 1978

Printed in Great Britain by
Cox & Wyman Ltd,
London, Reading and Fakenham

Contents

Foreword

To set the record straight, although this is by no means a book on our personal lives, it might be good to give a little background. My wife, Pauline, and I started our life of service to Christ in 1919, by joining C. T. Studd (her father) in the Congo. In 1931 we began thirty-five years at the home bases of the Worldwide Evangelization Crusade which C. T. Studd had founded. I was British, and then International Secretary. They were years for which we are tremendously thankful. We proved, with our many fellow-workers in the worldwide expansions of the W.E.C., that it is specifically in earthen vessels that God manifests 'the excellency of His power'.

For the past eight years, having passed on our W.E.C. responsibilities to other younger men, we have lived, with our daughter Priscilla, in a home the Lord gave us on the grounds of our U.S.A. Headquarters. I have spent my time very largely in house meetings and gatherings of all kinds all over the U.S.A. and Canada, where there are endless open doors and eager participants, sharing much of what I am writing in this book.

I gratefully acknowledge and extend my thanks to

Mrs Bette Ketcham and to Mrs Lorna Kerr for the typing of the manuscript. I am also thankful to my friends in Lutterworth Press who have published all I have written since the first on C. T. Studd in 1933 and with whom I have always had such excellent relationships: and on this side of the Atlantic to my own co-workers in the Christian Literature Crusade who undertake the distribution.

N.P.G.,
  Fort Washington,
    Pennsylvania, U.S.A.

Chapter One

Why This Book?

Why am I starting to write again? I will jump right in and 'tell it like it is' from the beginning. It is because years ago in my late teens dissatisfaction with my life and the challenge of a friend confronted me with what I had long been taught from the Scriptures – that I was eternally lost and deserved to be, unless I had received Christ as my personal Saviour. I did that the same night, and in my heart I had the inner witness. Because Jesus' blood had been shed for me, then my sins were forgiven and God was my Father, and I was going to heaven, not hell. A joy I had never known before was in my heart, and Jesus had become a living Saviour to me. *This* was life – eternal life. This was the answer to the meaning of life. But it was only the beginning of the answer.

I gradually began to find that there is a difference between the sun at dawn and the sun at midday, and I began a pursuit, like Lancelot and the Holy Grail. I wanted what could be a total answer for me, a full satisfaction, a rational meaning to all life, a fool-proof work-able key to daily living, a roadmap which I could unfold to a fellow-traveller and say, 'This is the way.' And for myself I daringly say the Grail has been found, and the midday sun does shine; and it is no longer a matter of searching, but of exciting fresh explorations of this 'Promised Land'.

Long ago the Psalmist asked, 'What is man?' And it is a fair question. The Greeks said, 'Know thyself': and let's face the fact – all we have is ourselves, and we had better know in the fullest way who we are and why we are, and how we can be ourselves and what our destiny is.

I have dug around these vital questions in several former short books, which are still – surprisingly to me – in circulation. They have been written over the past thirty years, and were an attempt to share what understandings I had at the time. It is not a question of wanting to take back what I then wrote, no indeed not, but only of, to me, increasing clarification. Truth is simple, that is why Jesus spoke so simply. The complications stem from our partial understandings and therefore partial explanations; and I hope this may simplify a little more what those other books have said – *The Law of Faith*: *The Liberating Secret*: *The Deep Things of God*: *God Unlimited*: *The Spontaneous You*. I have not reread them, and doubtless I shall repeat things said in them. I had better hide under Peter's umbrella: 'I will not be negligent to put you always in remembrance of these things, though ye know them and be established in the present truth'! And well I know we are mere paddlers in the ocean of the 'unsearchable riches of Christ', with hardly a toe in the water yet, as we shall surely realize when the day comes in which we 'shall know even as we are known'.

I like always to repeat and underline that the Scriptures have always been the final authority to me, ever since fifty years ago, when taking a theological course for my undergraduate studies at Cambridge, I was greatly disturbed at some of the liberal viewpoints which undercut the facts as related in the Old Testament; and I made a personal decision in my room, rather dramatically maybe, on my knees with my hand on the Bible, that Christ having become so personally real to me, I would stand without compromise on accepting the Scriptures as evidently He did. I haven't, by God's grace, changed nor desired to change in these succeeding years, but rather all the time see ever greater depths of the ultimate of revelation in them.

Chapter Two

There Is Another Dimension

So we start, and we shall start by taking a big leap. There is a spirit dimension, and there is a matter dimension. There is appearance, and there is reality. Paul puts it: 'The things which are seen are temporal; but the things which are not seen are eternal.' Commonplace and obvious? Yes, but revolutionary, because all our understanding of life is geared to the visible, and we are occupied by 'the sweat of our brow' and the application of our minds in expanding and using the visible. Anything not within the compass of our reason we consider crazy. But what do we find in the Bible? A continuous record of happenings which we call supernatural, which cannot be fitted into our interpretations of normal cause and effect. Abraham and Sarah have a child when respectively a hundred, and ninety years old; Joseph accurately foretells through dreams; Moses brings plagues on Egypt, crosses the Red Sea on dry land, gets water from a rock and daily manna; Joshua crosses the Jordan, and brings down the walls of Jericho, and stops the sun for a day; Elijah stops and then brings the rain; Elisha makes an axehead swim; Daniel spends a night among hungry lions; the three young men walk in the fiery furnace and come out without even the smell of smoke on them.

Jesus was continually doing things beyond natural explanation, bringing calm in a storm, walking on water and thus counteracting gravity (and Peter doing the same), feeding five thousand with five loaves, healing all kinds of diseases, and raising the dead. Paul and the apostles saw prison doors open, chains fall off, the dead raised up; and the writer to the Hebrews reminds the whole church in the famous 'faith' chapter 11 that these things were really so.

Now immediately I mention these things, you will tend to think I am pointing to specific remarkable happenings and asking, 'Why don't we see the same?' No, I am not. That is dangerous thinking, because it is centring our attention on dramatic incidents as if they are what matters; but the question I ask is, Do we not recognize that here are happenings which are products of another dimension, the spirit dimension, and altogether beyond the scope of human thinking and action? They belong to the absurd: or they belong to the real, and we are in the absurd who discount them and claim the only real to be our laboured efforts! That is all I am now saying. Not that we ought to be seeing things like these, though we must say they could be if they are the products of faith; but that there is a dimension of spirit, where He who is spirit, and we who are 'joined to Him one spirit', operate right in the midst of this matter world; and we discover ourselves to be spirit people, not matter people, with revolutionary effects on our whole way of seeing, thinking and acting; and that *this* is the truth, or we should rather say that He who is spirit is the truth. We shall explain as we proceed.

So the first great fact is that the whole universe is spirit. It doesn't look like that, and our first reaction is to question that. So let us start like this. We know what spirit is because the Bible tells us we humans are spirits. The writer to the Hebrews says we have flesh-fathers, but that God is father of our spirits, in other words our real selves (Hebrews 12:9). Paul defines our self, or our ego, as spirit when he says, 'What man knows the things of a man save the spirit of man which is in him?' And that in me which says I know, is obviously I, and that I is spirit. If we die in Christ, it says we are 'spirits of just men made perfect', our real selves having left its body shell behind. If we die out of Christ, we are 'spirits in prison'. Always spirit.

Chapter Three

Spirit Is The Only Reality

Now I myself, being spirit, am meaningless in relation to others unless I have a means of expressing my spirit-self; and that, in Bible terms, is my soul and body. My soul is my emotions and reason, emotions expressing my spirit-desires, and reason expounding my spirit-knowledge: and of course my body the means of out-ward contact. The simple evidence that we humans are spirit-selves, expressed through soul and body, is that if I meet a person, I don't say I met a body, but a person, because I caught on to the spirit-self expressed through the outer form.

Now this gives us a human jumping-off point to understanding Jesus' supreme word, when He said to the woman of Samaria, 'God is spirit'. There we have it. If God is spirit, then that is all there can be, and all must be spirit. If in the beginning, as Genesis says, there is only God, all must be some form of Him; and we know this is so, because we are taken to the end time by Paul in 1 Corinthians 15, when he tells us that after the last enemy is destroyed, the Son will render up the kingdom to the Father that 'God may be all in all'. If He is all, then everything must be forms of Him; and 'all in all' means He, The All, in all His forms of manifesting Himself.

We understand this from the fact of us humans being spirits. Just as we have a necessary form by which to manifest our spirit-selves, so He. The universe is He in manifestation. The universe is spirit slowed down to the point of visibility. Paul says that all men have an inner understanding of Him the Invisible 'by the things that are made'. The visible manifests Him the Invisible, so that 'things which are seen were not made of things which do appear'.

So we are saying one tremendous fact. There is only One Person in the universe. There is only God. The universe is God in manifested forms. We will develop that much more in a moment. But you see the importance. If all is He, we are to learn the secret that Jesus knew so well, of seeing through the appearances to Him the Reality. And we see the unity of the universe, the oneness of all, which is a present fact to the eye of faith, and is stated in its final form when Paul says that He is going to 'gather together in one all things in Christ'. That settles it. All is one, and that great day is coming when what now appears separated to the outward eye will be visibly and eternally one in Him. Think of that, not Christ in the universe, but the universe in Christ, proving again that all is one spirit. Even the word universe means one, and Christ's final prayer is on oneness. All through history people have had flashes of this fact of unity and it has a great effect on our consciousness when we begin to see through to this oneness now.

In the light of this revelation that the universe is this One Living Person, and everything and everybody is He in some manifested form, whether good or evil, whether positive or negative, this obviously raises some disturbing questions, when we include evil in the everything. This will become clear as we proceed. Suffice to say now that we shall never find the answers to life's problems until we see Him The Only One in all activity, not two powers but one. Not a dichotomy, but a unity. As Jesus said, 'If thine eye be single, thy whole body shall be full of light. But if thine eye be evil, thy whole body shall be full of darkness.' But the opposite of single is not evil, but double. Why then evil? Because to see double is to see evil. We only have the secret when we see as Jesus did, through all to one – to Him, the Father, including seeing through the devil. Isaiah saw this more clearly than any other writer in the Bible in some chapters such as 45 and 46. 'I am God, and there is none else . . . I form the light and create darkness: I make peace and create evil.'

Of course many times I am asked if I am a pantheist. I am not a theologian, and probably my questioners are not; but I had plenty of Greek in my English school days, and know that 'pan' means everything in the neuter case, and 'theist' of course a worshipper of God. But that is just what the idolatry of Romans 1 was, which lies at the roots of man's ruin – worshipping the creature rather than the Creator. That means calling the thing God. But what we are talking about is seeing through all things to the One of whom it is some form, just as I don't mistake a person's body for themselves; I see through the body to the person of whom it is the outer form. When therefore we humans have returned through Christ to knowing God as the Living One, our Father, then all life becomes worship, because our eyes are opened: we see through everything and every person to their being some wonderful form of Him in beauty, power, shape, texture, colour, in nature, in music, in the powers of sight, hearing and thought: though some may be outwardly distorted into ugliness.

But that raises another question of equal importance. If the whole universe is One Person, and what we produce is what we are, what kind of person is He? For the universe must be a representation of its author. Of course we know the answer, but how fundamentally important. John gives it. Jesus made that three-worded statement, 'God is spirit'. John makes the three-worded statement, 'God is love'. That is all that need be said. 'Is', not 'has'. If He is love, then He is nothing but love; and Paul said love fulfills all laws of the universe.

And what is love? In a word, love is for others. If I love, my interest and involvement is to meet the other person's need, no matter what happens to me in the course of it. And this is our God of the universe. He is love. He exists for His universe, not His universe for Him. If His universe is fulfilled, He is fulfilled. If it is happy and harmonious, He is happy. That is why He is safe as God. In all human history, because we are self-interested, not other-interested, all those who have power over others turn it to their own advantage. It is they for him, not he for them. That has been the curse of dictators, kings, rulers, tyrants, yes and capitalism – turning what they control to their own advantage. But God is love. It is not the universe for His convenience, but He for it. His pleasure is when we are pleased and satisfied. The final title given Him in the Bible is 'The Lamb', in the book of Revelation. It comes no less than twenty seven times. 'The Lamb on the throne': 'The Lamb is the light thereof': 'The marriage supper of the Lamb': 'Follow the Lamb withersoever He goeth'. Why Lamb? It seems curious to liken Almighty God to a helpless lamb; in worldly terms ridiculous. But what is the character of a lamb in the pasture? Helpless availability. You can do what you like with it. If it conveniences you to kill it, kill it. If to eat it, eat it. And this is the nature of God, only that He is deliberately, and not helplessly, available. He is love; if therefore to kill Him meets our need, kill Him. If to eat Him, eat Him. Which is precisely what He is in human history, the Lamb slain for us at Calvary. The Lamb eaten by us in His body and blood, as symbolized in the Lord's supper.

Chapter Four

The Son and The Sons

A one is meaningless except by differentiation from another. A universal becomes comprehensible to us by its particular forms. What is electricity? I don't know. But I know light, and heat, and power. That is manifested electricity. So the invisible God, whom Paul said, 'No man hath seen nor can see', as love would be self-manifested. He would come into visible form. So the first manifestation of Himself, as recorded in the Bible, is His 'only begotten Son'. He is the Father by the eternal begetting of the Son, who is given His full stature when it is said, He is 'the brightness of His glory, and the express image of His person': 'in Him dwelleth all the fullness of the Godhead bodily'. It is for this reason that only through the Son we can know God as the Father, as the Living Person. The Son, the particular One, manifests the universal One to us as the living Father. 'No man cometh unto the Father but by Me.' Those who seek a way to God, apart from the Son, cannot know Him personally. He remains impersonal to them, as in religions such as Buddhism and Hinduism. This indeed is the key when talking of God to those of other faiths or no faith. To them He is a theory or at best an impersonal entity. To us, we tell them, through our faith-relationship with the Lord Jesus Christ, His manifested Son, God has become our personal Father: as the Father of the Son, we know Him as Father. Experience is the best answer to theory. 'He that hath seen Me, hath seen the Father', said Jesus.

If, therefore, the first purpose in the begetting of His Son was to manifest Himself as who He is, and He has become His Living self to all who have believed in Jesus, then the next purpose has been revealed in the Son being the agent of the Father, 'by whom also He made the worlds'. We see that by the example of the founder of any world-expanding business. The founder cannot do the expanding. He has to have a second level of sons, executives, to establish the firm on a worldwide footing. So God's Son is His agent in creation, called in John by that curious term, 'The Word'. 'In the beginning was the Word. The Word was with God. All things were made by Him': and He was Jesus, the Word made flesh. But why called the Word? Because here we reach the central spring of action in a person. We will go into it in more detail later. But a person is a person because he has the capacity of decision; and persons being inner persons, spirits, the decision is an inner one, though expressed in outer form. And that is the spoken word. We say, 'I will do this', I will go there', I will make that'. Within ourselves our primary activity of thinking has crystallized into an inner decision which I express as a word. The word is I in action: I do, I go, I make, is the bodily form of that word.

Now what was that original word? Genesis tells us: 'Let there be light': 'Let the earth bring forth grass': 'Let the earth bring forth the living creature': 'Let us

make man in our image'. Just 'let there be'. And here is
faith in action in its first mention in the Bible. But why
'let there be'? Because we fallen humans, while we mistakenly regard ourselves as in such a distant relationship
to God, look on faith or prayer as a desperate means of
getting God to intervene in a situation. We call on Him,
or with a great effort put faith in Him, as if He was
asleep in our need and we must awaken Him to send the
supply! But the real truth is that He is awake and we are
asleep! He is busy awakening us by putting us in the
place of need. It has always been the Father in action,
the One with the eternal love-purpose of manifesting
Himself in some new forms of goodness. Like air
presses on us so many pounds to the square inch, so He
presses Himself through His sons, and not they getting
or arousing Him into action. The sons let the Father
through; and they do it by speaking the word of faith.
By that word, the Spirit brings the Father into some new
form of visibility. So, 'Let there be light, and there was
light', and 'The Spirit of God moved upon the face of
the waters'. Just as by our human word, our human
spirits go into action.

That is why faith is effortless, not sweating at it; for,
as we say, faith is not we trying to drag God on to a
scene to get Him to supply a need; that comes from our
illusory concept of God at a distance, and we by ourselves in a tough spot. But it is recognizing that He is
there with the supply before there is the need: 'Before
they call, I will answer'! We as sons speak that word of
faith, 'Let there be'; and the manifestation comes in His
way, not ours. Faith is as easy as that, and here in
Genesis we have its first example.

Now we come down to earth a little more and more

from the Son to the sons. In doing this we will take a leap, right through what we shall later trace as the history of the human race, and move right on to our destiny. We are told that in Christ we are the sons of God. This is an enormous advance. We are created sons, He is the Son in the deity. Yet, to fulfil God's purposes, He identified Himself totally with us human sons, and through redemption, lifts us to the level of co-sons with Him. He is spoken of as 'the firstborn among many brethren', as 'not ashamed to call us brethren,' ash 'in the midst of the church' singing praise unto God. But what does this lead on to? Paul's statement that if children, then heirs; we are co-heirs with Christ. But heir of what? It says God appointed His Son 'heir of all things'. The universe is His inheritance, and therefore ours. A pretty big inheritance! But what does a person do with an inheritance? Bury it, sleep on it, hide it? The parable of the talents warns us about doing that. No, we get excited if we receive an inheritance. Now there's something we can use and develop; here's a new opportunity for us. So that means that if the universe is our inheritance, we are owners, managers and developers of it. What a destiny! But it immediately spells vast responsibility. We can only manage something if we are fit to manage it. And what can make us adequate managers and owners of God's universe? Only one basic fact. If we spontaneously are 'gods', in the sense that we are in a unity relationship by which we are the same kind of person that He is, then we are love, as He is love; we are lambs as He is the Lamb; we have one nature – to be for the benefit and fulfilment of the universe we inherit, no matter what that costs us, and not our universe-inheritance for our benefit. That's all. Love fulfils all law,

23

all the principles of God and His universe. Inherent in love is power, wisdom, everything.

But a person must be a person in his own right. He must be himself and know how to conduct himself and how to manage his affairs. You do not appoint a person as director of a vast enterprise the day he joins it. He starts from the bottom, in the basement hammering nails, climbing up stage by stage till he knows by experience the business he is to manage. And that is the divinely appointed history of humanity. Life is serious, deadly serious. Life is responsibility. Life is involvement to the last limit; and yet the paradox is that that is total gaiety, continual fun, endless zest and excitement. Permanent gaiety at the heart of total seriousness!

Chapter Five

What Is A Person?

So now we move into the heart of things for us — what it is to be a person, and how I then function as a spirit-person in this matter dimension, both in time and eternity. This will take some examining, and we must not balk at any issues. How do we find and know ourselves and then be effective selves in all the distorted condition of human living? What is the fool-proof open sesame?

We must start at the beginning. First, what is a person? In ordinary terms, a person is a person because he is conscious of variety. He is a conscious person. We may say that there is a consciousness in the animal and vegetable kingdoms, and even maybe in the mineral; but what we mean by consciousness is our natural capacity of differentiating between variety and applying our differentiations. We may say the ant or bee has the highest level of social organization below man, but neither seek to improve their ways of living. They haven't that type of consciousness. But we live by examination, application, development. We are persons, as God is the Person.

How then do we express our personhood? By freedom of choice. Freedom is our key. The history of humanity is the continual outbreakings of demands for freedom. But let us carefully note what freedom is. It is not being anything or nothing. That is where such drugs as LSD have taken people, into an apparent freedom from everything, which turns out to be a total nothingness, a vacuum, being a non-person. No, freedom is the necessity of making choices. You have to choose. Life is always choices between alternatives. Freedom is the privilege of choice, but also the necessity of choice.

Where then does freedom lead to? Curious paradox – to bondage. That necessary act of freedom – making the choice – always results in the thing we take taking us. You take food, food takes you. Once you have swallowed it, it is your master! You choose a profession, the profession takes you over. You become known as a carpenter, doctor, engineer, airman. You go to a conference, you are controlled by the conference programme. So freedom is always bondage; but it remains true freedom because I freely chose what now controls me, and find my pleasure in my bondage!

The truth is often missed and is of great importance. It looks like freedom to be free to do anything. It actually must always work out that I express my freedom in making specific choices. My freedom then is the captive of my choice and I am enslaved by it. But I then fulfil my freedom in its true sense by my freely enjoying developing my choice. A doctor enjoys practising his medicine, a carpenter carpentry, a married person marriage, although in this distorted world it doesn't always work out so ideally in the pleasure we find in it! Free choice is only another word for what the Bible calls faith. (These Bible terms often need restating to put fresh meaning into them, which is the value of our modern translations.) So faith, defined as free choice, lies at the roots of personality, and indeed establishes its destiny.

Let us trace the enormity of that statement, and let us see free choice, expressed in words of faith and the actions that follow, as the royal robes of personhood, our innate autonomy, that which caused the Psalmist to say 'ye are gods', and in Genesis that we are 'in the image of God': but seeing also that choice leads to destiny, and the chooser becomes his choice.

It was a surprise and revelation to me when, after always seeing the many Bible statements on God as almighty, therefore able to do anything, and it being surely blasphemous to say that there is something God cannot do, I find the Bible itself contradicts itself (in our human manner of speaking). Twice over it says there is something God cannot do, and that is to lie. Not did not, or had not, but could not. That is strong language of God – 'that cannot lie' in Titus 1:2, and the same in Hebrews 6:18 – 'impossible for God to lie'. And here I saw the tap root of being a person, whether God or man. A person is only a person by being conscious of alternatives and being compelled to choose. And what is the ultimate alternative for a person? Being a person means I know I am myself and love myself and must fulfil myself. But there can only be one of two ways. Either I love myself by getting all I can for myself, indifferent to what that means to others, a self-getter, a self-seeker, a self-gratifier, or I love myself by wanting to be all I can for my neighbour, to satisfy him would satisfy me; my self-love would be fulfilled in self-giving. Either I am myself by getting all I can for myself; or I am myself by giving all of myself for others. And when it

27

says specifically that God cannot lie, I find what is the eternal choice which has 'fixed' Him. A liar is a self-getter. I lie to gain my own ends. And God cannot be that. What a tremendous foundation to this universe. The Being of all beings, the Person of all persons can only be the opposite to a self-getter: a self-giver. He is love, and everything that ever happens on this universe has as its source and completion the One who can do nothing but love. Everything, no matter what it looks like, is some form of self-giving love, for He cannot be anything else. That is our rocklike foundation. That is why, whatever happens, we sin the ultimate sin when we question what kind of God it is who permits or ordains that? That attitude will always be a darkness in our spirits. But if we say we cannot understand how that fits, but 'everything You do is perfect love', then the inner light shines. We are in tune with the Infinite.

And see the evidence that God as the Person in the universe is fixed by His choice. He *cannot* be the alternative. He is a love-slave; for it says of His Son Jesus, His express image, that 'He took upon Himself the form of a servant' (slave in the Greek): He came 'not to be ministered unto, but to minister': 'He ever liveth to make intercession for us', and as such it is the delight of His Father to give Him 'a name that is above every name' to which 'every knee shall bow': for this was His Son in human form expressing the total love-nature of the Father.

Chapter Six

The Origin of Evil

If, therefore, God is who He is because He is fixed, and fixed as love, plainly every person who is to find himself and be a person equally becomes fixed. We often hear it said that the origin of evil is an unfathomable mystery, but, unless I am mistaken, I have not found it so. It seems plain enough. First, we understand evil to be the term we use as the opposite of good. But, good is the term we use of God who is love, for all that love does is good. Thus Jesus, when called Good Master by the rich young ruler, said, 'Why callest thou Me good? There is none good but God!' So then, if good is the term used of the Living God who is the other-love, evil must be the term used of anyone who, as a person, is the opposite of God, and evil because he is self-love. Evil, therefore, is a person who, as a free person, has made the opposite choice to God and is fixed in it – a mis-used self rather than a right-used self.

This is why in Isaiah, God says, 'I am the Lord . . . I create evil.' The moment God creates persons like Himself, and, in no other way can He have sons to develop His universe, they can only be developing persons by their freedom of choice; and fundamental choice is, shall I be an expression of God in His self-giving love, or shall I, in my freedom, separate myself as a person (though, of course, eternally having my being in God) and function as a self-loving self? To be such, the opposite to the Self-giving One, would be what we call evil. Evil, therefore, is a necessary alternative in freedom. To be free involves the possibility of being evil. That is why it says that God creates evil. If He creates persons, He must create them free or they are not persons. If they are free, they can choose to become the opposite to Him in His fixed choice, and that is evil. Therefore, in giving freedom, God gives evil as a possible alternative.

And that, I think, is the eternal wonder of God's love in redemption, and the final revelation of the ultimate of love. In creating free persons, He created the possibility of the evil choice, yet He is not responsible if that choice was made. He could, therefore, have said, 'Well, they made the choice for which I am not responsible. Leave them to it, and let Us make another race of persons', which is what He told Moses at the incident of the golden calf to stir in Moses the love-response he must have to handle Israel at this crisis. Exodus 32:9–14, and 32:32. But love belongs to need. Love is the debtor and need always love's creditor, for need, as Paul said, has an inescapable claim on love, which exists to meet it. So God as love has to go that second mile. Responsible for freedom, but not responsible for that wrong choice made in freedom, He says, 'I will take the whole upon Myself, both the freedom for which I am responsible, and its wrong use, for which I am not responsible; and I will take that ultimate curse of that wrong choice upon Myself, and remove it in the blood of My Son' – the Lamb ordained to death before the foundation of the world.

30

So we know where evil began. It was the first free person, not of this human race, but of the angelic order, who could only be established in his unique appointment as 'the anointed cherub that covereth' (Ezekiel 28:14) by becoming fixed by choice as Lucifer, which means bearer of God's light. But, instead, he spoke his free word of faith which fixed him in self-interest, self-seeking, self-exaltation (Isaiah 14:13–14). Evil, therefore, had its public origin in a person who became fixed in self-centredness, the opposite to God. This was 'sin' which John explained as 'transgression of the law', law being the way a thing works; and the way the universe works is by Him who is love. So sin is a person who is self-loving love, just as righteousness is the Person who is self-giving love. Both are persons, for the universe is the Person, and we, as persons, His sons in the Son, Head and Body. It is in our separation from Him that we have come to speak of aspects of Him as things, as abstractions, such as goodness, love, power, peace, joy, etc., or alternatively of evil, sin, hate, envy, etc., whereas they are the Person who is these things. God is the Person. Evil is a created person who chose to be the opposite to God, and is called the God of this world because he brought into manifestation the opposite form of personhood. Sin is the root and sins are the product.

But what we are to note as we continue to trace humanity's history is that this evil one, called Lucifer, and Satan, is still and forever a rebel son, recorded in Job as among the sons of God presenting themselves to Him. He is still God's servant, though in rebellion, and still does God's will, and has his being in God, as all the universe had. This is important because owing to the illusory sense of separation from God which the Fall has given us, we find it difficult to recognize that Satan is not some separated person who goes about and does as he wills, and we have to, in a way, call on God to go and find and handle him. No, he is God's negative agent and we shall see how wonderfully he is God's convenient agent, and we learn to see through Satan to the One in full control of him, if we are to get all the distortions of life into focus. But again we shall look into this in more practical detail later on.

Chapter Seven

We Only Know Right Through Wrong

Now we come down to ourselves. We have seen God's purpose – to 'bring many sons unto glory', glory being to total fulfilment, a vast family of sons brought to their highest conceivable destiny as co-sons and co-heirs of the universe with His own Son. He had this in hand before the creation, 'according as He hath chosen us in Him before the foundation of the world', and this meant one thing – that the sons must be mature, capable sons, not a crowd of irresponsible little children, but knowing who they are as persons, knowing how to function as sons, and thus knowing their destiny and able to fulfil it. That means training and development from little children to sons, and thus to sons who can represent their Father and take over His business for Him. And this is the history of the human family.

There is one facet of mature experience which is often missed, yet it lies at the roots of capability on any level and none can be sure of himself and his proficiency in any profession without it. A thing is only a thing because it has its opposite. It has a right and a wrong, and the one had overcome the other. Sweet has overcome or swallowed up bitter, smooth rough, soft hard. Life swallows up death, said Paul in 2 Corinthians 5:4;

and it gets its strength from having an opposite which it has swallowed up. You cannot say a certain yes in a decision, until you have first canvassed the alternatives and said an equally certain no to each of them. The strength of the yes is in swallowing up the noes! Not in having no noes, not in ignoring their existence, but in facing them and replacing them by the final yes. Then only is the yes a strong and certain one.

Proficiency is not in ignoring the wrong way of doing a thing, still less in denying that there is a wrong way; but proficiency is in having known the wrong way and tried it out and learning once for all that it doesn't work that way. Then the yes has its strength in swallowing up its no. A carpenter, to be proficient, must first have learned that you don't use your chisel this way, or make your measurements that way, but then these are the right ways. No housewife can be confident in her kitchen until she first knows you don't cook that meat at this heat, or mix those ingredients in those proportions, then she is spontaneously at ease in her good cooking. And so through every conceivable activity of life. You must know the wrong way and have proved it wrong, before you are secure and confident in the right. The one must 'swallow' the other up.

And here we have God's perfect wisdom in the birth of the human race, and in having a convenient opposite, the wrong one, the evil one, through whom He would bring his vast family of sons to maturity. This was His first way of making the devil His convenient agent. To have sons, they must find themselves in their freedom. They must discover that to be a person is to be conscious that there are alternatives and make their free choice; and ultimately their right choice through having first

34

made the wrong one, and tasted the consequences. And the wonder of our perfect God is that He knew this was the way His predestined family of efficient sons must take, from wrong first and then to right; and He knew the suffering that entailed for them, with its possibility of a lost eternity. So he took it upon Himself to go that same way to its total final end, and in the person of His own Son, Himself in His Son form, to participate in the sufferings in their fullest measure. So Peter said we are redeemed 'with the precious blood of Christ, as of a lamb without blemish and without spot who verily was foreordained before the foundation of the world': and the writer to the Hebrews takes it even further by saying that this involvement to the full in the sufferings of humanity was the only way the perfect Father, to be perfect, could go so that 'it became Him, for whom are all things and by whom are all things, to make the pioneer of their salvation perfect through sufferings'. Tremendous!

So we find our first parents in the garden, and placed between two trees, one to give life and the other death. Why did not the Father just put them there conveniently with only one tree? It wasn't very kind of Him to put the two! We might just have eaten of the tree of life – and then been what? A crowd of helpless babies who knew nothing and could do nothing! No, the first parents of these destined sons must first discover themselves, learn their potentialities, misuse themselves – and then they are ready to be reliable ones.

And at that tree of death the deceptive voice of that 'old serpent, the devil' came to them, and what it did for them was to awaken them to discover what it is to be a self. Enormous awakening with its vast potentialities.

35

Thank you, devil. Through those tempting suggestions to have what *she* would like, Eve found she was a person! She had appetites in wanting to eat that fruit, with all that goes with them in making us vibrant humans. She had the awakening adventure of new discovery through sight when she saw the fruit was 'pleasant to the eyes', all the limitless avenues of exploration in the visual arts and sciences. And the awakened mind, the topmost of all, by which she would know the truth of things and at the end of the long trail would 'know even as we are known.'

Eve, as representing us all, could only find and know herself by being solicited to be herself for her own self-ends. But more than that. She took that dangerous step which cut her off from being what we were created to be, sons in spirit-union with the Creator Son and the Father, and thus sons of self-giving love. Instead, in chosen separation from God, she, her husband and we all, became self-loving children of the god of self-centredness.

We became misused selves. We had to discover and experience what it is to be a wrong self before we are conditioned to be a right self. We have to learn misuse before we can settle into right use. One Person became a real human and did not go that way, and that was God's Son 'manifest in the flesh'. But He, to be a person had to be confronted with the devil and come under the temptation of the 'evil' way of self-interest. By that means He found His human self as a self, with all its normal capacities and reactions.

Therefore we must say that Adam and Eve could have made the necessary discoveries concerning themselves by temptation without responding to it. They could have replaced the attraction of the wrong fruit by taking of the right one, as Jesus did by answering the devil with the word of God; but as they did fall, we need waste no time in theorizing!

So we partook of the tree which brought the human self into manifestation in the form it was never meant to be – the self-loving self, the evil self. Indwelt by the serpent-spirit of error, it appears as a rival and attempted conqueror of the human self in its true eternal form – indwelt by Christ as the self-giving self. It has reversed the true order in which the self-loving form is swallowed up and ultimately unknown to the self-giving form it becomes in Christ, and progressively in us as we find ourselves in Him.

This tree of death has divided between good and evil and put evil in the ascendency; but in so doing it has given us to drink of the full draught of its bitterness to fit us to reach out to the water of life. The tree of life, of which we are now able to partake, since that cherubim's sword of judgement which kept us from it, was plunged in His side instead of ours, puts evil back into good. It restores us from the curse of the divided two-power outlook to the single eye, by the glorious discovery of how God uses the evils of this world to His and our good ends. But that we explain more fully later.

We have become children of the devil, who, we say again, is quite simply the created being who brought into manifestation the potential there must be in freedom, of being the opposite to God; and if God is self-giving love and love is good, then Lucifer, Satan, is that opposite self-loving love, the evil which, if it had not been exposed, lies hidden eternally, 'swallowed up' in the good. And we have eaten by choice of that divided

37

tree, and participated in this exposed opposite. But by doing so, we have gone along a necessary road by which a person must know and reject misuse before being established in the right use. And here is the meaning of the Fall, and its value.

Chapter Eight

What Is God's Wrath?

But it is important to realize that there is a fundamental difference between the fall of Lucifer and the fall of Adam and Eve, our fall. Lucifer had made his ultimate choice from his centre, his spirit, where he totally rejected God and replaced him with himself. He chose to be his own god. But Eve was tricked by the serpent (1 Timothy 2:14). She did not intend to reject her Creator, but just to bypass Him with an act of self-indulgence, hoping He would not notice! Her sin was of the flesh, not spirit; and Adam merely followed Eve for the same reason. So, thank God, the human family are prodigal sons, and have never lost the inner consciousness of having missed the way, and knowing by the inner law of their being what they ought to be. Slaves of the devil, branches of the false vine, children of the devil, caught up in the devil's destiny, but not yet sons of the devil who by free choice become devils like their father.

For this same reason the Father revisits them in their disobedience, I always like that beautiful statement: 'They heard the voice of the Lord God walking in the garden in the cool of the day'; and because they were God-conscious, they 'hid themselves'. But it is our guilt that projects wrath on God, as if that was His chief characteristic, and which still so distorts our concepts of God as if He is a monster. Still our unenlightened eyes, including, I am ashamed to say, many liberal theologians, regard the Old Testament as the record of an avenging God, instead of the same unchanging God of grace shining through from the Garden of Eden, to the call of Abraham, and through Moses and the revelation of the Tabernacle of continuing grace, to the full sunlight of His grace in our Lord Jesus Christ. But the wrath of God is only manifest in those who have the wrong relationship to Him. It is not Him as He is, who is all love. But it is what He must appear to be to those who run counter to the law of His being. The wrath operates in them, not in Him. If I have a right relationship to an electric switch and turn it on as I should do, I get a pleasant light. If I defy any warnings and stick my finger in the apparatus, I get a nasty shock. The shock is what I feel within myself through my unlawful contact. So it was not God who hid from the disobedient couple, it was they who hid from Him. They projected on Him a rejection which was really in themselves. And this is the wrath of God. All He said was, 'Where are you, Adam? Come out from your hiding, I haven't changed.' And when they came, He talked with them, not in judgement and wrath, but in mercy. All He told them was that they would experience the inevitable effects of the discords self-loving self always brings on itself. Sorrow was what they would have, sorrow in the man's life, sorrow in the woman's life. Sorrow is an inner reaction, for we are inner people. It is our inner response to suffering. Because we have fallen into our false material concepts of life in its outer forms, and have brought about total disruption in our outer living by our grab-and-hold and dog-eat-dog activities, life is a continual suffering: wars, diseases, poverty, anxiety, wrongdoings, and we regard it as if those sufferings are our problems, and why does God 'allow' them? But we are on the wrong foot. Sorrow is our problem, for sorrow is our inner reaction to suffering, and we are inner people. Change our sorrow into inner joy, and outer sufferings are turned to praise.

So it was the Father's special mercy, not wrathful judgement, when He told them three times over that they would have sorrow. Why? Because sorrow would mean dissatisfaction with their earthly conditions, and desire for a better way. Thank God for sorrow. Thank God the world is restless, fermenting, dissatisfied, rebellious at its present conditions. That is its hope. That's the best thing the Father could predict for His fallen children: and thank God, behind the sorrow and at its roots lies guilt for not being what we know we should be. But that was not all.

From that first moment of the Fall and its consequences, there was the pronouncement of deliverance; and the deliverance is in the seed of the woman which would bruise the head of the serpent. God said to the serpent, 'I will put enmity between thy seed and her seed.' What is the serpent's seed? The take-over of the human family created in the image of God by a false father who would express his nature of self-centredness in them. Thus they would be the seed of the serpent. But they are still the seed of the woman, created in God's image, and into the woman's seed would come The One capable of destroying the works of the devil, and turning the devil's captives into His captives. And what is more, though He would come to do this in due time in

41

human history, in God's timeless sight He was already, in the remarkable phrase in Revelation 13:8, 'the Lamb slain from the foundation of the world'. Therefore, He was already the true Adam, the last Adam, progenitor of the new race, and could be found in spirit, as the mercy seat for sinners, from that first day of the Fall. He was so found by Abel and by the countless thousands who, like the seven thousand in the days of Ahab's apostacy God was pleased to tell Elijah, had not bowed the knee to Baal. Abraham rejoiced to see His day: Moses counted the reproach of Christ greater riches than the treasures in Egypt: Israel in the wilderness drank of that spiritual rock that followed them and that rock was Christ. So mercy flowed out from the Garden and has never ceased flowing.

So this first stage, downward, not upward, was the necessary preparation for that vast family of sons of God. By this they could learn once for all, and reject once for all, not to be fooled again, the wrong way before the right, the misuse of the glory of being created self before its right use. And it is as if God said to Satan, 'You have deliberately turned your back on Me and founded this false kingdom of the negative, the power of darkness. So now I will use you to my great ends. Through you I will bring to maturity my vast family of sons to rule this universe. When they have well learned the lie from you, they will be safe followers of the truth, and not be fooled by you again. They may visit you at times, while within your reach on earth, but they will never live with you again. Thank you, devil.'

Chapter Nine

The Total Remedy

We already know clearly enough the only way we could be rescued. We have the false god in us. It came as a revelation to me when I saw what I knew well already of the redeemed – that the Holy Spirit lives in us; but then also I read in 1 John 4:4 that if the Holy Spirit is in the redeemed, there is also a spirit in the unredeemed. 'Greater is He that is in you than he that is in the world.' And then when two verses later, John plainly names them: 'Hereby know we the Spirit of truth and the spirit of error.' So the spirit of error, the Satanic person, is in us before we are Christ's. That was new light to me, and a new orientation. Most of us think of ourselves as just our unredeemed selves until Christ comes in and takes over. We do not realize that we have working in us that 'prince of the power of the air, the spirit that worketh in the children of disobedience' which Paul says is true of all of us (Ephesians 2:2). He has so concealed and disguised himself in us as unbelievers, though it says that it is the god of this world *in* us who has blinded our minds, that we just think we are our independent selves. But the truth is that all humanity are vessels. We are containers, and it depends which God is in the vessel. In Romans it says we are either 'vessels of wrath' or 'vessels of mercy': those who either contain the god through whom wrath is our portion, or those who contain the Saviour-God through whom mercy comes to us. This greatly simplifies salvation, for it is merely change of Gods, not change of the vessels which contain Him. Or to use that other great illustration, we are either branches of the false vine or of the true. 'I am the true vine', said Jesus, therefore there must be a false one.

Who then can make this exchange? Who delivers humanity from its slavery to its false usurper and replaces him by the True Owner? Obviously a slave can't redeem a slave. There can be only one, and that the Owner and Creator Himself. He only has the right to represent the human race and do something which can include them all. That is why we safeguard the incarnation in our gospel. There is no point nor power in the death and resurrection of Jesus, unless He was God in the flesh, the author of the human race becoming a member of it to represent it. This is one of those 'supernatural' events, of which we gave examples on our first pages, which are not explicable in terms of human thought but issue from the spirit, not the matter, dimension. So it is no good trying to explain or explain away what issues from the realm of what we call the impossible, but we are to learn what is really the only actual. Human thinking is what has bound us to realms of time and space; for the true realm we must have 'the renewing of our minds', the 'new man which is renewed in knowledge after the image of Him that created him'.

The way in which this change of Gods has become a fact has of course held our fascinated and almost microscopic attention and investigation through the centuries.

And no wonder. 'Upon Another's life, Another's death I stake my whole eternity.' 'God forbid that I should glory save in the cross of our Lord Jesus Christ.' 'I was determined not to know anything among you, save Jesus Christ, and Him crucified.' We will put it in simplest terms to relate to what we have already said. Why Christ's death? We humans have got so physically minded that death to us always means the physical. But we who are believers know better. We know physical death is only the gateway to life after death. Where? Ah, that is the crux! The Bible makes plain that if we die a child of the devil, we continue on into the devil's destiny which is described in the terms of its supreme loss as 'everlasting destruction from the presence of the Lord and the glory of His power'. Therefore death for Jesus did not just mean the physical dying. If as the One who never was made captive by the devil and thus not under death's dominion, He accepted death on our behalf, then He would go after physical death where we would go, into what Paul called 'the lower parts of the earth', the realm of 'the spirits in prison'. And that is where He did go. Maybe that is why there was such reality in the cry, 'My God, My God, why hast Thou forsaken Me?' Supposing He didn't rise? He had to go this way by nothing but faith, as the rest of us.

But He did rise. There was nothing that could hold Him, because, though our sinbearer, He was not Himself a sinner under the law of sin and death. Therefore, 'quickened by the Spirit', He could be 'raised from the dead by the glory of the Father'. And what did He leave behind on our behalf? That is what is important to us. He left both the cause and effects of sin. The effects are our destiny in outer darkness, the consequence of the

45

curse of the law, the guilt, the condemnation, the weeping and gnashing of teeth, the worm that dies not and the fire not quenched. All disappeared from sight for ever, because He took them on Himself on our behalf, and then left them behind on our behalf when He arose. Therefore Paul said that in His resurrection we are justified; in other words, not merely forgiven, which might still leave a memory behind of the things for which we needed the forgiveness; but justified, meaning that we are as spotless, sinless, as the Saviour Himself; and all the past in memories of fact or dread of destiny are out of sight and out of mind for ever. That is the overcoming in the blood of the Lamb. Nothing can be held against us. 'Who shall lay anything to the charge of God's elect?' 'It is God that justifieth.' The shedding of the blood was the physical evidence of a life totally poured out to death, and therefore taking all with it that would come to us if we died.

But that alone, tremendous as it is, would not solve our problem or give humanity its release. The cause is our problem, the sin, not the sins. And we have seen sin to be the term used for the nature of the spirit of error who lived his sin-quality of life in his vessels and by the law of an indwelling spirit, he expresses himself through the human spirit which he indwells. Sins are the products, but the producer is the problem. And what salvation would it be for a human race indwelt by the spirit of sin and thus compulsively expressing his self-loving nature, to be released from the consequences of a sinful life, but not from the compulsive cause? We should just go on living as before. Therefore the Bible presents us with Christ's death in a twofold form – in His blood and in His body, of which we are continually reminded in the memorial Supper. And that is why in Paul's 1 Corinthians 10:16–17 reference to the Supper he speaks of our communion in the blood and body of Christ. But then he says we are one with Him and His body, symbolized by the bread; but he does not say in the same sense that we are one with him in His blood. The reason is that a person's blood is his very self. When that is shed, his life is gone. But a person's body is more external, more we may say his clothing. His blood, therefore was uniquely Him going that way of death for us, and in that respect we were not dying on that cross with Him. Rather we come to the foot of that cross and see the burdens of our sins rolled away into His tomb, as Bunyan so beautifully puts it. But we are His body. 'We being many are one bread, one body'; and in that aspect of Him on the cross, we are there with Him, crucified with Him, buried with Him, risen with Him. And what's the import of that? Because the body is the container of the spirit, and we humans have become containers of that false spirit of error, whose nature is sin, therefore Paul says that Jesus did more on Calvary than 'bear our sins in His own body on the tree'; he said, 'God made Him to be sin for us'. And that meant that in God's sight we were He, crucified with Him, and His body representing us had that spirit of sin in it. And then the glorious fact that when a body dies, it is separated from the spirit in it; and so when He died, Paul said He 'died to sin' (quite different from dying for our sins). His body, representing us who were 'buried with Him', lay in the tomb with no spirit in it – a human race delivered from that old false indwelling spirit of error. And when He rose, it was by the entry of another Spirit, His Holy Spirit. So when we are joined by faith to Him

47

in His death and resurrection, we are no longer vessels containing the spirit of error, but vessels containing the Spirit of God! That is a full salvation – from effects and cause, from products and producer. That is why only the incarnate, crucified and risen Christ can be the world's Saviour.

Chapter Ten

What You Take Takes You

And now we are back on what it is to be a person. My royalty is my freedom of choice. All is mine as I make it my own. Nothing is mine till I do. The whole world is reconciled to God in Christ. He came 'that the world through Him might be saved', 'not willing that any should perish, but all come to repentance'. But it is to 'as many as receive Him' that He gives the right to become the sons of God. So we come back to the exercise of our one fundamental faculty, the right use of which is the main purpose of our life on earth. Call it freedom of choice, or call it faith, it is the same thing.

We have already seen that the capacity and necessity of making choices is the basis of our selfhood, and how our choices take us over. So faith starts by conscious choice, conscious involvement, but goes on as spontaneous being in that choice. I sit on a chair by choice. It is a 'leap of faith', just as much in such a mundane detail, as in the great choices of life. A chair is available to me, it is desirable, and it looks reliable. That is as far as sight or human reasoning can take me. I have to commit myself, before I can prove it is a reliable chair for me. But then, having sat, the chair is now holding me, not I it, and I forget about it and just remain sitting.

Faith has become spontaneous being, I just am in a faith-relationship with that chair.

So we have been in a spontaneous faith-relationship with the spirit of error all our unredeemed years. Whether consciously or unconsciously we have been living our self-centred lives, under his dominion. But now we come awake. Through one means or another, the inner disturbances of guilt, the realization of the judgement of God, the sense of emptiness and purposelessness, the sins that have a grip on us, the impact of the preached word or background Christian teaching, or maybe some sudden crisis in our lives, has brought us to our senses. We call it conviction of sin. Its effect is disillusionment and disgust with our philosophy of life. The misuse of self has done its work. We have had enough of it. Now in our fundamental freedom, we would transfer our choice of faith elsewhere if there is an alternative. We would move from the wrong to the right, if there is a right. And that is the gospel. And that is why the gospel must be preached to those who have never heard it. Who can deliver and save us, when we can't save ourselves? There is no concrete answer in our human history except the One who came and did it for us.

But we can't prove a thing. We have the Scriptures, we have the witness of changed lives, but they are no final proof. They are only pointers. It is only when desperation drives us beyond reason that we will make such a leap as this – into the invisible. But we do. From our inner spirit-centre we make our faith-choice. We will take the risk and take Him at His proffered word – that God did send His Son, that He did die for us, did rise, is alive, and does fulfil the promises He gives.

And now what happens? The law of faith operates — that what we take takes us. And in this case it is a supreme event, because for the first time we have transferred our believing from matter to spirit. We have believed on Him who is invisible; and back comes the inner witness. 'The Spirit bears witness with our spirit that we are the children of God!' We *know*. We can't say how, we can't prove it, but inwardly we know. We have taken the first giant step from matter into Spirit-reality. Somehow He is my Saviour. He has loved me and accepted me. I have become a child of God. In the eyes of the world I am a fool. Who is this Jesus and this God? Where are they? What right have you to say they have become real to you? Get back to sane earth living. But we have moved from matter to Spirit, from unreality to reality, and nothing can change us.

The first inner evidences we have are for our personal benefit. We have peace: 'Being justified by faith, we have peace with God.' And as we have just said, we are conscious of being loved and accepted and receiving the gift of eternal life. They are the only first way in which the Spirit of truth could communicate the reality of Jesus and the Father to us. We have lived all our lives in self-interest, and therefore only what would meet our own selfish needs could reach our consciousness. Love always meets people on the level of their need. So God gives us His Son apparently just to meet our selfish needs.

But tucked away in that package of grace was something far more revolutionary. We are continually saying that God's sole nature is other-love, and the true evidence that any are His sons is that they are expressions of the Father. If He is love and now lives in them, then

51

they are love. And so this tremendous fact becomes real. It isn't just that we rejoice in finding ourselves loved, but we love. In Bible terms, 'The love of God – not love for God, but God's own love – is shed abroad in our hearts by the Holy Spirit who is given unto us' (Romans 5:5). We just find ourselves, not by self-effort but by spontaneous inner compulsion, not just loved, but lovers. We can't help ourselves. We find we are loving Him who first loved us like that and gave Himself for us, and the Father who sent Him. And we are not only saved, but saviours. Having found at last what true life is, we can't but pass it on to others. And we are not just healed, but healers, as others share their hurt and we can give them Jesus.

This is why the Bible gives first place to the new birth. Jesus, Paul, John, Peter, all talk plenty about it. It is the moment of the settlement of our eternal destiny. It is the central transference of our capacity of free choice from attachment to the false god of self-centredness to the Living God of the universe, the God of love. Satan had no right to us. He was a thief and a usurper. God has the right to us because we were always His from the beginning, but had become lost sheep. So when He gets us back, it is for keeps. We are fixed through our union with Jesus in His death and resurrection. And again we say, the supreme evidence is that we have spontaneously begun to be, not just loved-sons, but lover-sons. We are the God of love in our human forms – true sons.

And the other important fact is that we have begun real living as spirit people, not matter people. Spirit, His Holy Spirit, has become real to us, making the Father and the Son in the realm of the invisible living persons to us. Now we have begun to recognize matter as shadow and spirit as substance. We have begun what is going to be the main progress of our lives, learning how to function as sons of the fourth dimension in the environment of the third dimension: how to settle in to reality not being of time and sense, and not according to 'normal' thinking; and how, as we have already seen in the lives of all the men of God in the Bible, this substance is manifested in this shadow realm.

Chapter Eleven

The Self Can't Be Improved

Our great error is in thinking that our human selves can be improved. And we think that because we have this false concept of being separated self-developing selves, this is false deception from the spirit of error. But in Christ we are not separated. We are in an eternal union. That is what, we were crucified with Him, buried with Him, risen with Him, means. That is the symbol of the Lord's Supper, eating His flesh and drinking His blood. From the moment we received Him, we were restored through Him to the eternal union, which I prefer to call unity, because union keeps the attention on the two, whereas unity settles us in the realization of something eternally indivisible – which is the fact by grace.

The relationship in this unity is positive and negative, so that all the illustrations given in the Bible point to that. We are branches in the Vine. The branch is the negative means by which the Vine can bear its fruit. But it is a unity, and when we see a vine we really only see its straggling branches and we call that the vine. The branches are the vine in their branch forms, and we are Christ in our human forms.

We are called the body of Christ. The body is the negative to the head, by which the head goes into action.

But head and body are a unity. So Paul called the body Christ in 1 Corinthians 12:12.

We are called the temples of the living God, the buildings in which God may be seen; and we are the earthen vessels whose treasure is the Christ within. Temple and vessel don't illustrate the unity, but do make it plain that they are merely negative containers, and we don't look for change or improvement in them.

So then how does this all work out? First, by a recognition, which is a revelation, that the human self by itself can only be motivated by its own self-interests; for its only true place in creation is in its unity with God, as the means by which He manifests Himself in other love through our human selves. Apart from our destined place in the unity, we can only be self-loving selves. Therefore it is useless and a waste of time for us to ask God to make us loving, or patient or pure, or free us from human reactions of hate or fear or worry or depression. It is asking an absurdity and an impossibility. The human self can never change. The vessel can never be the living water it contains. The branch cannot be the vine.

When that recognition is a reality to us, then we can start by accepting ourselves in our weakness and all normal human reactions. In this distorted world we are besieged all day long by fear and doubt and hate and worry and all the rest of them. To feel them is normal, not wrong. We shall always be responding to them. We hate or dislike this person. We are jealous of that one. We are afraid of what we are called on to do. We are worried by daily problems. We have fits of deep depression. Our minds are assaulted by all kinds of wrong thinking. If we struggle against them, what help is that? If we condemn ourselves for such reactions, we remain still bound and full of guilt. If we call on God to help or change us, we don't get changed, or maybe just a momentary relief.

Then on what grounds can we accept ourselves? Because of this great revelation: we are merely the negative joined to the Positive. We are no longer we, but Christ in us. Christ the real we! Listen to Paul. He starts by saying Christ died for us, then speaks of the Lord with us, and goes on to his special revelation of Christ in us; but he ends up, when he gives his personal witness, by Christ is the real I. 'I live,' he says in Galatians 2:20. 'No,' he corrects himself. 'It is not I, but Christ living in me.' Christ not with, not in, but replacing Paul, Christ in Paul's form. And Christ in your and my form. Put your name there. You are Christ in Jack's form, Christ in Elizabeth's, form, I, Christ in Norman's form, and so on.

Now, in the light of this revelation, when we in our humanity are moved in this direction or that by our negative reactions, we don't struggle, we don't condemn, we above all don't try to change ourselves (trying to be good is the worst sin); no, we *replace*. We transfer our inner believing from what has its hold on us because we are believing in it, fear, lust, hate, etc., and attach our believing to who we really are, not our human selves, but Christ in ourselves. And as we affirm and recognize Him, He who is the peace, love, courage, purity, manifests Himself in and by us.

There is the secret – discovering who we really are. We have come back home at last as the branch in the Vine and the Vine in the branch. 'Abiding' in that John

15 chapter is, in the Greek, just 'remaining'; and we remain by simple faith-recognition. The negative to God the Positive, and necessary as a negative, for only when we are consciously weak, as Paul said, then His strength is perfectly manifested. When we are fearing, He is the courage. When we dislike, He is the love. And Paul goes as far as to say he personally takes pleasure in negative situations of weakness, hurts, needs, problems, for when he is weak, then he is strong.

There is no doubt that this is the biggest tie-up in thousands of God's people; in fact all of us have to start tangled to get the knots untied. We are just so bogged down in taking ourselves for granted as normal functioning people, and we are so used to preserving an image, that it is a second spiritual breakthrough for us to grasp the fact of helplessness. We had come to acknowledge that we had not kept God's law and were guilty sinners. But it is another thing, when we are the Lord's, to discover and admit that we are also helpless saints. We can't do it, and not only can't but are not meant to. We call that the second collapse.

That is the whole meaning of Paul saying we can have dominion over sin, because we are not under the law. This is why there is that important chapter of Romans 7, which has been such a ground of puzzlement and controversy. There it is sandwiched in between the two victory chapters: in Romans 6, in Christ's death we are cut off from the former control of the spirit of self-centredness, 'dead to sin'; in Romans 8 we are joined to Christ in resurrection life, by His Spirit replacing that former spirit in us. Then in between comes Romans 7, saying we are not only dead to sin, but dead to the law. Why? Because if we are to function as living sons, we must know once for all in what sense our human selves can be manifestors of Christ. So Romans 7 is the human self which now has God's Spirit and delights in His law in the inward man, and wills to do it, and serves the law of God with the renewed mind. But self, when regarded as just by itself, has the virus of independence and self-reliance which Paul calls 'the sin that dwelleth in us'. That is the Satanic spirit of self-sufficiency which he calls sin. So the moment we humans, not yet recognizing Christ in us as the only keeper of His own law, want ourselves to keep it, and slip into this old habit of thinking we can do it, then down we fall. We can't do what we would, and do what we should not. Oh wretched man! And the law of God stands there to demand of us that we keep it, if we think we can! Then at last it dawns. Our human self is now a container of Another Self, Christ, the Spirit of Christ. We never were meant as humans to keep God's laws of self-giving love. Left to our human selves, we can only be ourselves and love ourselves. But this is just why Christ has come into us – to replace that evil spirit of self-centredness by which we had lived. By ourselves, we would still remain self-loving selves, but we are not ourselves any more. By inner union, Christ is our real self. So what do we now do? We tell the law it is no good its shouting at us, because we can't fulfil it, were never meant to; but we contain the One who can and does. So the law has not a thing more to say to us or demand of us. We are 'dead to the law' in Christ. And now we are free by simple recognition that Christ in us, Christ as us, keeps his own law in us, so that 'the righteousness of the law is fulfilled in us' who are now walking by inner recognition of the Spirit, and not recognition of that old self-effort.

How thankful I was when, as a young missionary, longing to be 'improved' – to love more, have more faith, the Spirit said to me, 'Drop that. You can never be improved. You are just a vessel.' And then He showed me that simple fact that God *is* love, not *has* love, and I saw for the first time that love is a person, God Himself; and that it was not a matter of my being made loving, but of me being the vessel which contained Him who is the love. I learned then to change from the false idea of becoming something to containing Someone.

Chapter Twelve

Separation Is Illusion

Now, as we move on to what is probably of most interest to most of us – how to live our lives as sons of God, there is one outstanding issue none can avoid. It is obvious from many of the biographies of the Bible, and the experience of thousands, including myself, that there is a second crisis of equal magnitude to the new birth; and it is not to be lightly passed over as in the category of 'there are many crises, and many blessings'. Without going into detail at the moment (we do later), anyone who reads the lives of these men of the Bible, sees how these crisis experiences alter their lives: Abraham at the announcement that he was to have a child in the impossible:[1] Jacob at Peniel:[2] Moses at the burning bush:[3] Joshua, the morning after he had sided with the eleven spies:[4] Elisha at the rapture of Elijah:[5] David at Ziglag:[6] Isaiah in the vision in the temple:[7] Jesus at His baptism:[8] the disciples at Pentecost:[9] Paul in Arabia:[10] (though it is also true that the moment of crisis is not so plainly traceable in some lives: Joseph, Elijah, Daniel for instance).

[1] Genesis 12   [2] Genesis 32   [3] Exodus 3   [4] Numbers 13, 14
[5] 2 Kings 2   [6] 1 Samuel 30   [7] Isaiah 6   [8] Luke 2   [9] Acts 2
[10] Galatians 1

We need to go thoroughly into the reason for this crisis because it so vitally affects our own lives. The fact that as a human family we are matter people rather than spirit people has trapped us in a great illusion. It is that we see reality in terms of separation, not unity. Everything and everybody appears to us separate, this here, you there, and so on. Physical science has already considerably shaken this outlook, by which we have now learned (though not so to appearance) that matter is a vast interflow of invisible particles, radiation, vibration, the wave theory and the quantum theory, and so on. Yet obviously we live our lives by a relationship to matter and people in their separate forms.

What then has happened? If God is spirit, and the universe is in fact He manifesting Himself in all outer forms, then we should be see-through-ers to Him in action, rather than see-at-ers, as if the external is the reality. Obviously Jesus, as perfect man, was always seeing through and bringing into visibility health in place of disease, calm instead of storm, life instead of death. The trouble has been through our perverted believing. Motivated by self-interest from the Garden of Eden onwards, we have believed in the reality of things and people in their outer forms and acted on that basis, because we wanted to hold and get and handle the outer world for our own benefit. It is our false believings which have put the distortions and disease into our world. If we had not fallen, we should have been servants of all instead of grabbers of all; and in loving and serving, we should have been in harmony with the loving and serving Spirit of the Creator, and we should have been seeing through and co-operating with Him in and through all. The outer world should have been merely the representation of the inner. And this is how, since being reborn of the Spirit, we have begun to act by the new through-look.

But having this matter outlook in life has had severe effects on the way we look at ourselves and God. We have seen ourselves and Himself in separation, not unity. We start, even at our new birth, by seeing Him 'afar off'. Yet Paul most strikingly says that as a whole human race we are always meant to discover that our very being has always been in God. A bold and radical statement! He never has been afar off from us except to our illusory misunderstanding. In his Athenian speech in Acts 17, he says that God had made all men of one blood to dwell on the face of the earth, 'that they should seek the Lord, if haply they might find Him, though He be not far from every one of us: for in Him we live and move and have our being'!! Surely the destruction of our false concept of separation!

However, the fact remains we have lived in this sense of separation; and as I say, even when we have first met with the Lord at our new birth, we still think of Him as apart from us, and therefore, of course, with the sense of our apartness from Him. And here is where our problem lies, and why there has to be in the experience of most of us a second crisis, resulting in a new dynamic relationship.

Our difficulty is not so much how He relates to us, as how we relate to Him. That is where the failure lies, and of which we are so conscious in our newly sensitized selves. It is we who seem to come so short. It is our unlikeness to Him which bothers us. Frankly, we are disgusted with ourselves, downgrade ourselves, even hate ourselves. If we don't take condemnation for the past, we do for the present! And this is excellent. All along we have said that if we are to be the sons we are meant to be, we must know ourselves and how we fit into the picture. The whole purpose of God in our human history is that first we discover ourselves, and then learn the difference between being a wrong self and a right self. Then we can be the sons of God.

Our trouble is that we have lost sight of the basic relationship between God and His universe, including ourselves. The best way I can put it is the interrelation between positive and negative. I have already touched on this a little, but we now need to see it very plainly. A positive and negative are the two sides of the same thing: light and darkness, smooth and rough, love and hate, sweet and bitter, and so all down the line. The one, the positive, is the thing. The other, the negative, is the lack of that thing. Light is no-dark, love is no-hate, smooth is no-rough. And the negative is only observable where the positive is not in operation. Yet the positive is built on the negative. There is no such a thing as the one without the other. Love is only known as love, because there could be no-love. Sweet is only known as sweet because there could be no-sweet.

The perfect relationship between the two is that the positive has 'swallowed up' the negative, to use the Bible expression we have already quoted – 2 Corinthians 5:4 or 1 Corinthians 15:54; or in the sense of 2 Corinthians 12:9: 'My strength is made perfect in weakness.' And Paul says the same in 1 Corinthians 11:19: 'There must be heresies among you, that they which are approved may be made manifest among you.' But what Satan has done, by making his free choice to be the negative to God's positive, is to expose the hidden negative, and

63

make a falsely operating dimension or kingdom out of it. Instead of being Lucifer, the no-light by which God's light is manifested, and thus being what his name says, the Light-bearer, he chose to be his own light in his negative self, the false light of self-love; and thus he broke away from the Positive-negative union for which he was created. He became what we might call a phony positive, expressing his created self by itself and for itself, as being its own light; and as Jesus said, 'If the light which is in you is darkness, how great is that darkness.' So by this means he made what were to be the hidden negatives such as no-light, no-sweet, no-love, into aggressive false positives, so that no-sweet is 'positively' bitter, no-light 'positively' darkness, no-love, 'positively' hate. This is what the Bible calls 'the power of darkness'.

Now the consequence of this on us as a fallen race has been to deceive us into thinking that we are false positives, separate independent people, self-relying, self-developing, self-sufficient. And we can and do operate as such. But in doing so, we can never be more than self-loving selves, because our human selves are the have-nots and are-nots so far as self-giving love is concerned. Only the One Self of God, the Positive, is the self-giving love of the universe expressed through our negative human selves.

In our actual fallen condition we have been negative vessels, containers of Satan in his functioning as a phony and therefore self-centred positive; but he has so impregnated us with his false outlook that he has deceived us into regarding ourselves, not as Satan-indwelt, but as separate, self-running selves, and we have thought of ourselves as such.

Now, used to this independent outlook as separate selves, when Christ comes into us, we have partially given up our independence, insofar as having Him as Saviour and Lord; but we have carried with us this false sense of separation, and thus still being our 'positive' selves, self-acting, self-developing, though now with the Holy Spirit to 'help' us. (Help is a dangerous word for us, for it has a false connotation.) We have no concept of being God's negatives. Union or unity are strange words to us in our world of separation. We know by grace the Holy Spirit who had borne witness with our spirits; but we don't know about being joined to the Lord, one spirit.

The result is that we think we are to become Christ-like people. Somehow we will begin to love God and our neighbour. We shall become patient, pure, good. We shan't be controlled by our dislikes of people, our hates, jealousies, worries, depressions, bondages to habits, fears. We want to 'be like Jesus'. We will to be. We try to be. We ask God for help. We regret and are ashamed of how we come short. But we shall surely improve! Shall we? Never!

As before, God uses the wrong to condition us to find the right. This is how all these men of God I mentioned earlier ran into years of frustration, and were finally cornered, usually by some crisis event; and there the light dawned. Abraham could not get the promised child by his barren wife: Moses could not rescue the Israelites by his own great human abilities: Jacob could not escape the vengeance of Esau: Elisha could not find that secret of Elijah's power with God: Job could not argue his way through to justify what had happened to him. But each in their travail came to the birth.

Chapter Thirteen

Have We Two Natures?

Again let us get this straight. This is not that old confusing and mistaken idea that we humans are possessors of two natures and in a struggle between them, dog eating dog. This is the error which puts us into the continuous condemnation of 'we ought to be different'. Cut the words 'ought to' out of our vocabulary. They belong to the law which says you ought, and the law He has 'taken out of the way, nailing it to His cross', and has 'abolished in His flesh the emnity, the law of commandments contained in ordinances'. Negatives are the opposite end of their positives, and their only 'nature' is to express the nature of their positive. So we humans have not natures of our own, but we express the nature of the one who lives in us. Of old, as the old man, we expressed the nature of 'the spirit that worketh in the children of disobedience' so that we were 'by nature children of wrath' according to Ephesians 2:2–3. As the new man in Christ we are 'partakers of the divine nature' (2 Peter 1:4), which is the Spirit of God bearing His own good fruit by us.

Our confusion may be because I may feel it is all very well to talk of Christ living in me, but in practical fact, far more of me shows up than of Him! And it is all very well to say I was once a partaker of the Satanic nature of self-centredness and expressed him; but now I am a partaker of the divine nature and express Christ. But do I? Or if I say I have put off the old man and put on the new, it seems to me lots of the old man is still very evident! But that is where we need to get this 'two nature' question sorted out, and this old man – new man syndrome.

The confusion is between centre and circumference. The centre is the set of our lives, the circumference is what may temporarily influence us. In our old life, in 'the old man', our centre was fixed, we being owned of the devil. We were slaves to him, Paul said in Romans 6:16–22. Now a slave is the property of his master; but no one can take from him his basic freedom. So we may imagine a slave serving his master all day, then when his master is away somewhere at night, the slave will exercise his freedom by a visit to the market. He still remains a slave, but just goes his own way for a short while and returns to where he belongs. So now a slave of Satan can go and do a few good and religious things for a time, but that doesn't change his basic slavery. So equally a slave of Jesus can be tempted to exercise his human freedom in the ways of the flesh and does so, but back he comes to whom He belongs.

We are what we are at our centre, and our nature is the nature of the one who lives in us at the centre. A temporary deviation does not alter that basic nature, but is just a diversion. When at the new birth Christ becomes our fixed centre, we have begun to express His divine nature, though we may and do deviate into the flesh; but that does not alter the centre. So just as a slave of the devil can do a few good things occasionally and return to whom he belongs; so a slave of Christ can do a few bad things and return to whom he belongs. Do not mistake a deviation for a nature. We can never have two natures at once. Impossible. We are always pure at the centre, in the sense of the word meaning unmixed. We were unmixed in our heart allegiance to Satan; thank God we are now unmixed in our allegiance to Christ. You cannot have a double mind or double tongue (as James said of a fountain not being able to 'send forth at the same place sweet water and bitter'). We have a single mind or tongue, but it can be temporarily diverted. Call that double, if you like, but basically it is single.

Chapter Fourteen

The Crisis Experience

But it is one thing to know truth by being taught it, by seeing it in the Bible, or by mental grasp of it. That is a right start and we do not despise it; but the reason we stress the second crisis, call it by what name we like, is that being inner people, life is lived spontaneously and naturally only by a fixed inner consciousness. We are in outer life what we inwardly know we are. In our former life, before we were Christ's, we had a consciousness, though maybe a vague one, just of being ourselves, and so we lived on our self-level. Then after we had knowingly become children of God by the witness of the Spirit, we had a new fixed inner consciousness: we were now forgiven, loved, accepted, inheritors of eternal life, we were in living relationship with Jesus and the Father; and without any special effort this had its radical effects on our daily attitudes and actions.

But this was still a gap-consciousness. Here we were, and here was Christ with us or even known as in us.

But that is something different from a full and final union-consciousness that we are He in our human forms: not we living, but He living our lives, as Paul said; and Jesus even said that we are the light of the world, not having the light, but being the light. How

69

could this be on any other basis than an inner unity, for He is the light, we the negative non-light? Yet here He is saying we are the light! Now this is the third level of consciousness, inwardly imparted as a fixed certainty, whether accompanied by outer signs or not, and given many names to label it, a consciousness of inner permanent unity as fact, never again seeking Him as if apart from us, the experienced unity-relationship of branch and Vine, body and Head. And when there is the inner consciousness, then we are just this. All we ever have to do is recognize it and act on the glorious fact; and because it is our fixed consciousness, it has spontaneous outcome in our daily lives.

For this reason we stress this crisis experience, because, both in Bible and post-Bible records, most of us do not settle into a given consciousness and new power in life until by some specific means, and usually a dated moment, we know that this is so. We see the same in what we call our 'conversion experience'. The Bible never says you must be able to point to a given date; but you must be able to say it is a given fact! Paul had a dramatic Damascus road conversion. When we do not know inner truth we may think such an outer experience is necessary. I thought so in early years. 'If Jesus would appear to me like that, then I could believe Him,' I would say. But of course it was not the shining of an outward light which blinded Paul, those with him saw no light and lost no sight; it was the inner illumination in his spirit which was his conversion. And I talk with those who cannot give a date or dramatic account of meeting with Jesus, and they get disturbed and begin to question about themselves then they hear the stories of these sudden conversions. Such disturbance is good;

for we must know either by a reaffirmation of a former saving faith or by a new act of believing. All that matters is my ability to say with Paul, 'I know whom I have believed' and with the blind man, 'whereas I was blind, now I see.' The fact is essential, the date a detail.

As with the new birth, so with the union relationship, there is a meeting with God by the Spirit, for most of us in a crisis experience, which permanently affects our inner consciousness; and we move out into a spontaneous life of liberty, authority and fruitfulness. How this takes place we want to examine more thoroughly, as well as its outcomes; but first we shall look a bit more closely at some of the men of the Bible to whom this happened. We can only glance at those great moments, sometimes with a little that preceded it and sometimes with a little of the aftermath, where we wish we could give more detail.

It was only after some years of walking with God in a faith life, that Abraham had that meeting with God over the birth of a son in the impossible, which finally fixed him in faith on a permanent basis; and Abraham was at ease, not only in the 'miraculous' birth of Isaac, but years later in his faith for a physical resurrection when told by God to kill his son. Abraham walked those years in a different dimension.

Jacob at Jabbok was named a prince with God which was the meaning of his new name Israel. From that night on he knew he was God's royal son with God's resources at his free disposal. He was no longer a fearful and persistent suppliant for God's favours. He was now the established patriarch. When young Joseph appeared like a foolish young megalomaniac with his boastful dreams, his father could see through and 'observed the saying'; and when introduced to Pharaoh, the world's greatest potentate, though a homeless immigrant dependent on Pharaoh's beneficence, 'Jacob blessed Pharaoh'; and 'without contradiction the less is blessed of the better.'

Moses we all know at that burning bush. But see the difference. Before, a beggared exile, stripped of all those human resources of the royal household which had caused Stephen to record that he had been 'mighty in word and deed', a fugitive for forty years from the Pharaoh he was supposed to have forced to release the Israelites: now, suddenly, surely a crisis moment, he inwardly saw something (for no mere outer eyes would have seen this desert bush which burned and yet was not consumed). He 'saw' that God is no distant watcher over human affairs, but is Himself the doer by His human agents. God was that fire whose fuel was the common desert bush, and Moses was such a bush! And that meant God in such realized union with His human agent, that He directly told Moses he was both a god to Aaron and a god to Pharaoh, and could act as such; and there followed the plagues that broke the power of Pharaoh, and the opening of the Red Sea, the water from the rock, the daily manna, the face to face communings with God on the fiery mount which was death for the people to touch (who still knew only a God at a distance); and Moses was called God's friend, and his face shone with a light which made it necessary for him to wear a veil. This was the man at the bush.

Look at two more, Joshua had a near shave (as we all do!). He had some warning lessons on the dangers of his special form of self-sufficiency as an able general. It was not his military skill, but Moses' raised hands of faith which defeated the Amalekites. As he descended the mount with Moses and they heard the revellings of apostate Israel round the golden calf, Joshua's proud military mind interpreted them as the noise of battle where his prowess would be needed, whereas Moses knew them for what they were, the lewd songs of the idolaters. While the people remained in the camp under judgement, Moses, who knew well enough the failure they had been, mingled daily with them, but Joshua hid himself away in the tabernacle, 'holier than thou': and when Moses summoned the elders to meet with him, the Spirit fell on them, but also on two elders who had not obeyed the summons but remained in the camp, Joshua was indignant for Moses' authority, and thus by implication for himself, and called on Moses to rebuke them. Moses' simple, selfless answer was, 'Enviest thou for my sake? Would God that all the Lord's people were prophets, and that the Lord would put His Spirit on them!'

But then the moment of truth came to Joshua, the cornering we all have, to bring us to our final awakening. Joshua was among the twelve spies who returned from their visit to the promised land with a report on its natural abundance and bringing the grapes of Eschol; but who also brought their terrified and unbelieving account of the giants who made them feel like grasshoppers, and the cities exaggeratedly said to be 'walled up to heaven', in the usual way belief in evil always exaggerates. Only Caleb of that twelve rejected their report and alone spoke that great word of faith, 'Let us go up at once and possess it, for we are well able to overcome it, and as for the giants, they are bread for us.' But Joshua, for the last disastrous time controlled by his human military judgement, had sided with the eleven.

That night was his 'second crisis'. Next morning, when the people were so frenzied with fear that they talked of stoning Moses and Aaron and electing a leader to take them back to Egypt, it was not only Caleb, but now Joshua with him who aligned themselves with Moses. Joshua that night had 'died and risen with Christ', as we would say. He entered into that same union relationship with God as Moses at the burning bush, for a few years later when God was taking Moses to Himself, He said to Moses, 'Take thee Joshua, a man in whom is the Spirit, and lay thine hand upon him.' And Joshua could, in greatest calmness speak those words of authority which opened the Jordan, brought down the walls of Jericho, stopped the sun for a day, and settled Israel into the promised land.

It took Elisha eight years, after his total initial commitment to God by giving up his prosperous farm to follow Elijah, to discover that commitment is not the same as having authority with God. Evidently Elijah had a secret hidden from Elisha; for he could talk about standing in the presence of God and telling Ahab there would be no dew or rain until he himself, not God, said so: and he could call down fire at a given moment after a day of taunting the priests of Baal. What kind of man was this? And now the Training School students were maliciously warning Elisha that his leader was about to leave them as he said he would, and Elisha was his successor. So what? Elisha was cornered. He had to get through; and do any of us get through till we have to? And he did, for again he 'saw' as only the prepared do see. 'If you see me when I am taken from you', Elijah said to him, 'That will be the moment when you see what I have seen all these years'. So Elisha stuck by Elijah and would not leave him, and saw him taken up in a whirlwind; but as he did so, he saw way beyond a man being raptured, he saw the One with whom Elijah had been at home those years, 'the Lord of hosts', the One with the endless resources. So Elisha found the secret and was at ease in it. He could raise a sunken axe-head and make it swim, he could cross a river, raise a dead young man, purify poisoned food. The plainest evidence was when Elisha had been giving away the secret plans of Israel's enemy Benhadad king of Syria, and the king sent his army by night to surround the small city of Dothan where Elisha was. In the morning, his servant was terrified. There was no way of escape. 'Alas, master, what shall we do?'

'Don't look outwardly at man', Elisha said in effect. 'Lord, open the young man's eyes that he may see', and he saw 'the mountains filled with horses and chariots of fire round about Elisha' – the Lord of hosts with whom Elisha was now at home.

To these we only have to add the two mountain-top experiences of the New Testament: Jesus before and after His baptism and the coming of the dove, and the disciples before and after Pentecost. We all know the difference.

Chapter Fifteen

The Charismatic

So we are saying there is a break-through in our consciousness to a union with God, call it by whatever name
– baptism of the Spirit, fullness of the Spirit, entire
sanctification, full salvation, the victorious life, entering
into His rest, enduement with power, rivers of living
water, the second blessing, the second work of grace.
And we specifically mean by that, not an in-and-out
relationship by which we have to find Him, call on Him,
regard it as though in the events of our lives He is
looking on, or has to be asked to take over and deliver us,
as if there is always a gap between us which has to be
bridged; and this, mind you, is the normal way we believers talk about our relationship with Him. We ask the
Lord to bless. We ask Him to take something over. We
ask Him to be present as if He was absent. That is not
the relationship we are talking about. We mean a consciously imparted recognition of unity, such as we have
just seen exemplified by these men of the Bible in their
whole change of understanding of how things are between them and God; and their consequent simplicity
and boldness of authority in functioning as God. This is
different.

Yet this is the real relationship of every redeemed

person, for this is redemption – the restoration of the union relationship in which the Father is living His life of love-in-action through the free personality of His sons. In the human dimension, fathers and sons are externally separate persons. But not so in the Spirit dimension. It is the Father in the sons doing the works, as Jesus said of Himself: 'The words I speak unto you I speak not of Myself: but the Father that dwelleth in Me, He doeth the works': and 'as He is, so are we in this world'. It is the dissolution of that external separated concept which the unity-consciousness ensures.

I know I run into difficulties and disagreements when I speak of a second crisis, and in any way seek to give evidence that such is needful. My difficulties lie in two directions. One from the many Bible-centred brethren who strongly oppose any second experience beyond the new birth. We have it all in Christ, they say, and all we need is a gradually larger understanding of who we are in Him and He in us. The other is from the many brethren, especially these days, who rejoice in the second experience but claim that it has the necessary outer evidence, as at Pentecost, of speaking in tongues.

Now what I personally think is closest to the minds of the New Testament writers is solely the reality of our in-Christ relationship and the Spirit-filled life which is the outcome. The means is secondary, also the timing or the occasion. It is wholly right and wholly Biblical to say that, in the finished work of the Saviour by His death, resurrection and ascension, and the coming of Spirit, all was completed for ever, and there is not a thing to add to it; and it is all ours the moment we have entered by faith into the saving relationship with Him. I believe that wholly. The moment I am justified by faith, that same moment I am unified with the Father and the Son by the Spirit. I am there and then eternally a branch in the Vine, a member of the body joined to the Head, a vessel of mercy, the temple of the living God. I am sealed by the Spirit until the redemption of the purchased possession. I am sanctified by the offering of His body and perfected for ever. I am endued with power from on high and filled with the Spirit, and baptized by Him into the one body.

My need therefore is not to have more, but to possess my possessions. To know who I am, not who I ought to become. Not to acquire, but to recognize. Therefore I am saying that it is possible, and may be actual in some, that there is no second crisis: they entered in to all at once. But that all means all, which includes the inner witness of the Spirit to the fact of the union: the liberation of the walk, free from that unsatisfactory 'up and down' living of Romans 7, and its constant conflicts: living the life of Romans 8, which is 'rejoicing evermore, praying without ceasing and in everything giving thanks': consciously and continuously filled with the Spirit, not dry one day and fresh the next, not cold one day and on fire the next; knowing and using the enduement with power as a royal priest in the service of a needy world: for all this is in the simplicity of the eternal union. All I can say is that I certainly did not know this fullness when I first came to Jesus and gave Him my life. And I am sure thousands are like me. But I did find this secret later.

There are the many, all over the world today, who with the spread of the charismatic movement rejoice in a new experience of God through the gift of tongues, and usually speak of it as 'the baptism'. They number millions in all nations, and are the widest-spreading branch of the Christian church of today. To me it is regrettable that also many in fundamental evangelical circles reject these manifestations as spurious. There are various shades of opposition. There are those who call it Satanic: others regard it as divisive: others suspect it as being mainly fleshly demonstration. Then there are those who do not oppose it, but are more fearful of what they think are its dangerous extremes than being thankful for what God is doing by it. I am among those who most thankfully see in it another of the great outpourings of the Spirit in the history of the church. I have known personally so many whose spiritual life has been transformed through receiving this gift that I know it is of God. No people love Jesus more and give more glory and central place to Him, and therein I would be like Paul who said, 'Every way, when Christ is preached, I do rejoice, yea and will rejoice.'

We know there was plenty of tongues in the early church, from the start at Pentecost, which meant that all the apostles had received the gift, through to Paul who thanked God that he spoke in tongues more than them all, and wished all did. We know of it in the Ephesian and the Corinthian churches, yet it was so commonplace in the birth of the young churches that we are not told of the Corinthians speaking in tongues until later when Paul had to warn them against excess. I see no ground or right to attempt to relegate tongues to those first years of the church, and misuse the statement in 1 Corinthians 13:8 that tongues shall cease, which of course refers to the coming final day when we all know Him face to face.

I would rather say that the gift of tongues, which is

what is usually meant when the brethren speak of having 'the baptism', is a means by which the Holy Spirit gives a sudden convincing, supernatural, and glory-filling inward confirmation of the union of spirit with Spirit, and of the fixed indwelling of God. In other words, it may be the quick way in which God does bring many into the experience of His fullness. It may also be, and there is a good deal of evidence of this, that their experience has overshot by a long way their understanding of what this life in God involves; and just as the Epistles expound what Pentecost was all about; so there is much room for mature Bible teaching among the charismatic brethren. Some have said, 'Some have come the slow way and learned en route what road they are on. Others have taken a big leap quickly and now need to study the road map.'

But the problem arises when more importance is placed on the means than the end. This is common with all of us, but outstandingly so with the charismatic brethren. One root of the divisions between the sincere-hearted among God's people is the ease by which we have strong convictions of the truth of some form of doctrine or experience. We then claim conformity to this to be as necessary as the simple central reality of our faith, where we are all one, the person of the Saviour Himself. We have the danger Paul warned the Colossian church against of 'not holding the Head'. Maybe we, who are His, do acknowledge our ultimate basis of unity in being 'all one in Christ Jesus'; but the strength of our conviction that some particular interpretation of some Scriptural truth, combined with the joy we have in it, and the fruit we see from it in our particular fellowship, gives us a dangerous bias. It may cause us either to state categorically that none have God's fullness unless they have it along our way of seeing truth, or at least that those of another viewpoint come short of all they should have. It is true that there is and should be variety of interpretation and conviction. This is the evidence of vitality in any human concern; and we are each meant to put all we have behind our special insights. We should each have a spiritual bee in our bonnet, but not that it should buzz louder than the bonnet. Only, by this means has new truth come to light or forgotten truths been revived.

God's subtle wisdom in the Scriptures is that they are not a systematic theology, or we should quickly be caught in this very trap of making more of the ways to climb the mountain than of the mountain itself, more of our attempts to understand Him than of Him Himself. That is why the delight of the Epistles with their varied authors is that they consist of the personal outpourings of their hearts and minds to meet what they saw to be a special need of some special group of believers. It is left to us to dig and extract the treasures of eternal truth from them, with plenty of scope for various mining operations for various precious metals. There has been room for Calvinism and Arminianism, for different emphases on holiness teachings, for variety in forms of worship and church order, for the structured and the unstructured, for the established churches and the Jesus communes. But always with this one danger lurking round the corner – of the over enthusiasm which centres my attention on my special brand of revelation at the expense of my recognition of the unity of all who are in Christ. Even the Bible can become more to me than the Christ of the Bible, forgetting that 'the letter killeth and the Spirit giveth life', and 'the words I speak unto you, they are spirit and they are life'. Truth is The Person, we are one in Him, not in Biblical interpretations of Him.

Again we say that there is a rightful place for concentration on that aspect of truth by which He is most His living Self to me, and to go all out for sharing it. There should be local loyalties. There is a place for an exclusiveness where those who see the same can worship and witness together in harmony and fellowship. But can we do this without that virus working in us of believing and implying that ours is *the* truth? Can it remain *a* truth among truths, and *the* truth only being Jesus Himself as way, truth and life, and the oneness and rightness of all who love Him? The unity of the body of Christ is not something non-existent which has to be built in our day. It always has been. We *are* one. In the outward healthy diversity: in the inward, where we are our true selves, unity.

But back to the charismatic brethren, the reality of their experience of the Spirit and the fact that tongues was common in the early church does cause them in a particular way to give the impression, and often both believe it and say it, that tongues is the necessary evidence of the fullness of the Spirit. To be filled you must have spoken in tongues. 'This only is the baptism in the Spirit.' The main body of us believers can find no Scriptural evidence for that. The simplest proof is that the Bible never says so. Also that, though tongues was much in evidence in the early church, in all the epistles by all four of their authors, only one mention is made of the gift of tongues, and obviously no special interest shewn in it as something of importance in the churches, still less of it being a necessary experience. It is only mentioned in the famous First Corinthian chapters in which Paul warns against its overuse.

There are the gifts of the Spirit as well as the fruit of the Spirit, many of them mentioned in Romans 12, Ephesians 4, 1 Corinthians 12 and 14, and 1 Peter 4, as the Spirit's equipment for the church in the world; and tongues is one of them mentioned by Paul. It is good and right that all who receive gifts from God should use them in their right place, and tongues has been given both for personal worship and public use. It is evident that all the gifts of the Spirit were in common use in the New Testament churches, when the brethren 'came together' in fellowship. But in most of our present church-fellowships, we have become so frozen in our fixed forms, even distributing in print how we are going to spend our 'worship' hour (and woe betide us if we go over the hour!), that no room is left for the autonomous expressions of the Spirit. To speak in tongues in such 'services' would be so startling that it would inevitably draw attention, disturb, even frighten some, and probably cause division. Therefore those who want fullest liberty in praise and worship along full New Testament lines usually meet in separate congregations. But praising God by any of the gifts of the Spirit, by the lifting up of holy hands, by the use of all kinds of musical instruments, by clapping and even dancing, are all there in the Scriptures; and thank God, new liberties in worship and freedom in fellowship, and even in expressing love one to another, are breaking through among many of our former structured congregations; and may they do so more and more! No wonder the youth of today crowd into charismatic meetings! They want an outlet for their enthusiasm for Jesus, instead of in the night-clubs or dance halls. There are those now who are finding their freedom in fellowship, where each can be himself in the Spirit. Each can worship, praise or pray in the way God leads him, without one judging the other, the one as too vocal or the other as too silent! For they are occupied with the Lord and not with each other.

So, as we grow in maturity, we can number among our own fellowships the quiet and the more vocal, those who have and use a special gift of the Spirit, and those who don't. This for years has been the basis of our co-working among the 1,200 of us in the Worldwide Evangelization Crusade and Christian Literature Crusade.

Chapter Sixteen

Faith Becomes Fact

But now to return to our main line on the second crisis. There are those who do not accept the need of it and have entered into the fullness of the union without it; and there are those other brethren who have had their distinctive second crisis in the 'baptism' with tongues. But what of the many who, though Christ's, know their need of this conscious union and the fruits of it, but do not have it in experience, of whom I was one?

The way to realization is not one iota different from the one way. There is only one way – whether for entering, for fullness, for effective living and service – what the Bible calls 'the law of faith'. We have said again and again that faith makes the insubstantial substantial, which is what Hebrews 11:1 says: 'Faith is the giving of substance to things hoped for, the evidence of things not seen.' Faith makes something real to me, though it may have been real all the time and real to others. Faith is my individual freedom, my autonomy as a person, to attach myself to what I want, to what is available, and what seems reliable. Therefore behind faith is specific desire. Faith works by love. All my actions are inwardly motivated, that's why I do them.

In the things of the Spirit we have already had our

first proof of what I am saying. By the inner operation of the Spirit you desired salvation. You had been presented with Jesus as available. You counted what is said of Him in the Bible as reliable. So you took the inward plunge. You inwardly spoke the word of faith: 'I receive You. I believe in You. I believe that here and now You give me what You say You do – forgiveness of sins, eternal life, the right to become a son of God.' And you spoke that word of faith, either to yourself by yourself, or with others in prayer, or by some specific means. It was a specific word. It was a leap, a committal, because you had no final certainty until you first did it.

And then what happened? This time, because as we have already said, this was your first leap from matter believing to Spirit-believing, you had no external response to your faith, such as you do when you sit in a chair, or go some place. But you did have that which you are now learning is your first touch with the real real! Within you, the Spirit bore witness with your spirit that you are a child of God. You can't say how because it was not a material evidence. It was simply an inner consciousness, assurance to your real self, your inner self, that Christ is your Saviour, your sins are forgiven, God is your father, heaven is your home. That is the substance that your faith gave you, and the evidence of the unseen now seen by you. And it has remained with you, because it was the beginning of eternal life, an eternal relationship. Certainly it has resulted in outward change of life, old sinful habits gone, new attitudes and conduct; faith without works is dead, but faith has been the evidence.

Now move that on this further stage – to this second crisis. Once again we start with quickened desire. We have not made our Christian living work, there is a missing spot somewhere; we have neither the power for service, nor for consistent living, nor for the inner rest from strains, nor ability to handle our problems. We have neither love for God, nor love for our neighbour, nor love for the Bible and prayer as we should have. What can we do about it?

We are told in simple Bible terms that the answer is Christ, not just as our Saviour and Lord, but our life: He being the real we, Christ in our human form, Christ is we. We may have varied explanations of what this means, or maybe no explanation. We may or may not know of such terms we have already listed such as full salvation, victorious living, the fullness of the Spirit, the baptism in the Spirit, entire sanctification, power for service, the second blessing, or union with God, as I have put it in these pages. Anyhow by one means or another we are prepared to make this second leap of faith – desirable, available, and apparently reliable – and settle it by this second word of faith: we say He is our all in all; He and we are joined in one spirit; He lives in me now, not I; He is the fullness, the power, the rest, the all I need: and that this is a fact now. Amen! We speak again that word of faith in our own terms. And it is now a fact in me, as much as He becoming my Saviour by my word of faith was a fact.

But now we have to watch out. Once fact is a fact, we have to avoid all temptations to look and see if it has happened! Which of course is really doubting the fact! We shall see later that this is a fundamental law in all acts of faith. That does not mean that we shall continually live in ignorance of it being a fact. But it means that the way and time in which the fact becomes a realized fact to us is not in our control. In the outer world the time may vary. We sit on a chair, immediately it makes itself known to us. We feel and see it holding us. Faith has become substance, the act of sitting has produced its own evidence. But some things take longer. We involve ourselves in learning a trade or language. It is equally a word of faith. We should not have started our studies without the faith that the trade or language is available and would be ours. But it may take quite a period before what we have taken takes us. As a missionary I know that. It was one thing to take by faith that I would speak that African language. The proof I believed, of course, was that I set out to learn it. It seemed to escape me for months. But then one day, I can remember the day, I just found myself speaking it. What I had taken had taken me! So with this 'taking' of Christ in the fullness of union. With some there is the immediate evidence, whether inner or outer. How? That's not for us to say. But somehow it has become a settled fact, and no further questions have to be asked. Plenty of questions on how we live in the light of this fact, but no further question on the fact. With others, as in my own case, it was a time (for me two years). But it did come: no, *He* came in this realization of the permanent union. Lots to be learned about it since, but no further crisis of this total kind. The union was settled, the replacement of me with Him at the centre, the union seen to be the unity, with the enduement and authority of the word: 'I said ye are gods, to whom the word of God came' (John 10:35).

So we need to get this clear. There is a response to our committal of faith. We are not left without witness, because the meaning of faith is that it gives substance to things hoped for. God does make Himself known to us, for that is His purpose, which leads on to the permanent intimate fellowship with Him, 'as a man speaks with his friend', so that we are at home with Him, understand His ways, and are co-operating sons. This could not be if faith merely meant that we reached out to Him – and blank in return! There is that 'full assurance of faith' it speaks of in Hebrews 10:22; but the snare is either questioning whether I have the fullness or trying some-how to get it. It is God Himself by one of His many means, external or internal, who confirms our eternal union. If you cannot say you are sure, nothing has hap-pened which gives you that certainty, very well, then, for the present be without the consciousness, but not without certainty of having spoken that word of faith which always brings substance. Stand on your word, based on His word. 'He that shall come will come, and will not tarry'; but meanwhile, like Habbakuk, you 'stand upon your watch, and set you upon your tower'; not so much to watch, as to affirm, praise and recognize the fact by faith.

Chapter Seventeen

Another Level of Consciousness

But then let us get this clear if we can receive it. These are our first halting steps in living in reality. And reality is the invisible, not the visible. We join Moses who 'endured as seeing Him who is invisible'. We have lived all our lives in the false habit of believing in what we outwardly see or feel as the real. It is a tremendous revolution to begin (what we did begin, as we have said, at our new birth) to live in the Spirit-dimension as real: He, Father, Son and Spirit as the only eternal real, and we by infinite grace in Him as body to Head.

And in this present second crisis of faith we are moving forward to a totally present-tense faith. Not now that He took away our past sins or gives us assurance of future eternal life, but that He only IS, and we ARE in Him in the Spirit, and that this only is the real. Therefore even when He has given us evidence of our union relationship, we are now moving into a consciousness which must not be confused with feeling – this subtle difference between soul (feeling) and spirit (reality). When a thing is, it just is, and all we do is recognize it and act on that recognition. We are selves for instance. We don't stop to ask; Am I a self? Am I here? I just am, and act on that fact! Now our eyes have begun to be opened to the one eternal fact – that HE IS ('I Am that I Am' was the name by which He revealed Himself to Moses), and to this the added fact that WE ARE, in this eternal union with Him in Christ.

Put it this way again. You can't know a universal. It is all there is. God is all there is. You may only know particular forms by which the Universal manifests Himself. So He gloriously and graciously manifested Himself in Jesus. But Jesus told His disciples it was necessary that He leave them in His physical form, so that He might come back to them and they find their eternal relationship to Him in Spirit. But Spirit is God the universal, and now in Christ we have moved back to union with Him the universal. And we don't know a universal, we can only be part of it. So in that sense we do not know Him on the outer soul-feeling level, and still less on the matter level. We just ARE in Him and He in us, and our consciousness is on that deep indescribable Spirit-level; as I say in the same sense in which we don't know ourselves, we just are ourselves, and that is the basic fact of our being and living.

I wonder if that makes sense to you. I am getting at the fact that it is good that we go through periods when we lose all 'sense' of God, all sense of Him being a personal living Being to us. We are in the divine dark, as the old Mystics used to call it, dark with excess of light. Dark meaning that spirit is dark to matter and vice versa. So God being spirit, we don't know Him and feel Him by the same faculties by which we know and feel matter things. It is another level of consciousness, in which we are – He is, we are – eternally. And to settle in that, we have to go through educating periods where we have lost all outer sight or feeling of Him. Then we don't get all fussed up if we are not conscious of His presence or feel Him unreal to us or absent from us. We are not any longer living in that matter-believing dimension. We are because He is, and we a part of Him, as a branch is part of a vine. And there we walk at ease and in confidence, for 'if I make my bed in hell, Thou art there'; indeed the Psalmist in that Psalm 139 puts it as well as anywhere else in the Bible.

But now here comes the paradox, which almost seems like a contradiction of all I have just said. Living in a visible and material world, really the world of shadows (just as in Hebrews it says the tabernacle ritual was 'the example and shadow of heavenly things', of which Moses was capable in the Spirit of being shewn 'the pattern in the mount'), God does manifest Himself of course. The whole world is the manifestation of Himself. Therefore He does have ways in which He makes us know. There are the outer ways of answering our faith in the symbols of baptism and the Lord's Supper. There is supreme provision in the written word. There are the outer signs, the Spirit coming as a dove to the Saviour, and in 'the cloven tongues like as of fire' and the speaking in other tongues at Pentecost.

Yet we also know these are meaningless unless they are the outward stepping-stones of faith which lead to the inner witness of the Spirit. So there is and must be this inner witness, whether accompanied by outer symbols or not. But then we are saying that even this necessary inner witness, which confirms our faith, is only the gateway into this final wonderful fact of being. This oneness of the union, when we have been taken beyond the need of witness to spontaneous being.

An outward illustration which I have already used

gives us some clue to what we mean. We sit on a chair by the act of committal (faith). The chair then bears its witness to us in that it is holding us. That is the substance of faith, and the evidence of its reality. But after that, we just forget we are sitting on a chair. We just are in that practically unconscious faith-relationship. That is about the best, though only partial way I can indicate by matter illustration what we are talking about in the Spirit-union.

Chapter Eighteen

Be Yourself

Now how does this work out in daily life? That is the common question, and the person who asks that usually means, 'Not well'. And that goes to the core of what we have been talking about. When the change-over has become fact, from the life which we were seeking to live with the help of God to a life which we inwardly know is He living it, then we simply don't ask that question. Why? Because something has happened. Previously, though we were Christ's, our self-reactions in daily living were what was most real to us. We were accustomed to assessing life by how we had behaved and we were usually unhappy with our failures and sins. We definitely saw it as starting from where we are and what we are doing, and proceeding from there to where Christ is or is not in it all.

But now turn it round the other way, as it is turned in our new consciousness. There is an underground river flowing in us. It is that the real I is not this human I at all! It is He, of whom my I is an outer form. There is a unity, fixed, eternal, inwardly realized, in which He, the Positive, is the Real One living, and I, the negative, am also real, but really the expression of Him. Now the curious effect is that it is very much I living a human life in all the hurly-burly of human living, yet that is no longer my primary consciousness. Here I am with my ups and downs, my ins and outs; I deal with them as they arise, yet they don't upset me or occupy my thinking and usual self-condemning as they used to. I have moved over from a self-consciousness in the centre to a God-consciousness in and through my daily living self. I have begun to live positively, overflowing the fact of my negative human self.

This is the new spontaneous living. Not one iota new in my environment. I am precisely who I was and where I have been all these years. But I am inwardly new in my consciousness, and, as we have been continually saying, we live by our inner consciousness because we are spirits, inner people. And in my consciousness I have moved over from my negative self with its negative reactions being my chief concern, to Him, not as some separate Self sometimes in charge of me and sometimes not, but as my Permanent Identity.

So normal Christian living, as Watchman Nee so well names it, is this 'mysterious' combination of the duality in the unity, the Positive and negative which alone makes manifestation of the Positive possible. It forever remains a duality in the unity, the Positive remains the Positive, the negative the negative; the one never becomes the other, the creature never becomes the Creator, or the son the Father, or the human the Deity. But the Positive-negative at last settle back into their right proportions. It is Satan who got them out of proportion (though God determined it for good purposes) by making us, the created negatives, as if in our self-activity we were positives. It is Christ who has restored the balance in which both God and we are real selves;

but it has taken the full restoration into the conscious unity for us to function in the healthy recognition that we are negatives, yet necessary to Him the Positive.

So this means at last that we accept ourselves. We have been busy enough being ashamed of ourselves, even hating ourselves, afraid to expose ourselves because we so falsely thought we ought to be and wished we were different. Miserable living! But now we laugh at ourselves, accept ourselves, love ourselves, because we have made the great discovery that we are meant to be precisely what we are. And watch that! What I now am, physically, materially, in my human make-up, in my present situation however much I have often wished it was different: equally in my relationships with others, family, business, workmates, neighbours: and, very important, including what I have been in the past which I may regret and which I may feel accounts for what I am in the present: in all this I totally accept myself as being God's precious person and He meaning me to be what I now am. And I praise Him for myself! I love myself! If I am a strange one, then I am His strange one, and He has taken me all the way, including my 'lost' years.

Paul got that right when he said that it was God who separated him from his mother's womb and then called him by His grace: and brother Paul had certainly been a deviationist, with his obsessive self-righteousness, and his violent opposition to the Christ of God to the point of murdering the Christians; yet he is here saying that God was in all that. He surely accepted himself, past and all! It does not mean that he justified himself in his past, no, that is the very thing he did not do, 'sinners of whom I am chief' was what he wrote of himself; but he so gloried in being the sinner justified in Christ, that he could look back and see that his very sins give him the background for his glorying in the grace of God and being able to meet fellow-sinners on their own level. His past was his compost-heap, as my friend Louise Mohr puts it, in which all the rubbishest rubbish becomes the richest fertilizer! So beware of this compulsive non-acceptance of ourselves which always means non-acceptance of others, for we love our neighbour if we love ourselves!

And now I live my daily life. Free. I have accepted myself because He has not only accepted me, but put me back where I belong as being really a form of Him. Now I am no longer busy, certainly not trying to find the One who has found me, but not even fussing around trying to hold on to Him; because He has got hold of me, joined Himself to me, and what He holds, He keeps. So why busy myself with anxiously clinging to Him? What a waste of time! No, no. I'll be myself, and it's up to Him to do the keeping. There is a curious sense in which we forget Him and just live. Why? Because life is forgetting ourselves, or rather transcending our self-consciousness by immersion in our interests or duties. That's what normal living is. We busy ourselves in our daily occupation. We certainly are not spending our time thinking about ourselves. That is why people turn to alcohol or anything which takes us out of ourselves.

So now, where Christ is our Inner Self, we are to forget Him! We are no more to spend our time looking in to find if He is still there or why we do not 'feel His presence' more, than we are to stop every half-hour to be sure that we are here! And that even includes special spiritual exercises such as 'the morning watch', or Sunday morning 'church' or Bible study. If we love a person, we surely want to know all we can about Him; therefore, we use all the resources available. The main resource is the Bible.

Personally I am thankful I felt in early years the need to study my Bible. I gratefully came to the conclusion that the Bible only came alive to me when I concentrated on a passage long enough for something in it to light up to me. That came most easily when I began to use a pen and to put in my own words, in a wide-margined Bible what that passage was saying to me; also when I was compelled to get into it by having to teach others. However, having said that, it still remains a fact that our permanent union-relationship with Christ is not dependent on reading the Bible. Abraham was the father of us all, yet he had no Scripture to sustain his believing; and the early church only had the Old Testament and that not for daily reading!

And the same with prayer times. They are the general title we use for communion with God. I was accustomed through many years to special morning times, often battling with sleep and wandering thoughts, and it was good discipline. But of course I have learned that prayer means fellowship times with God out of love of being consciously with Him, at any hour of the day and anywhere; and having faith transactions with Him over special needs (for which some use prayer lists); but I must safeguard myself from thinking that my relationship is more living with Him because I have had such times. There are those who say their day is never so good unless they have 'met with Him' in the morning. If so, it is the effect of things on our believing, not of His unchanging presence, which makes the difference.

What do we do, then, in our daily living with all the

variety of experiences which stream in on us – children, house management, business and work conditions, difficult workmates, injustices, things that go wrong, worries about security for the future, health, social activities, church duties, Christian witness? First there are whole periods of our daily living when things just run normally and we get on with them, or we are in normal contacts and conversation with others. Those are the spontaneous areas when we *are* Christ, without our knowing or thinking about it. We just are the light of our world. It is hard for us to get used to thinking of God in normal human situations. We have built up, through our guilt complex, this awesome idea of a God afar off who may be reverently approached on a Sunday morning, or some such. But God must be a common person if He lives in common you!! Hardly anyone saw the living God in Jesus. They just saw a man who did unusual things. Yet it was God manifest in the flesh. 'If you have seen Me, you have seen the Father', said Jesus. Yet He ate, slept, carpentered in his early years. Jesus, God? Why isn't He that carpenter's son we knew for years with his family? So we have daringly to get used to being ourselves, quite forgetful of Him as we are busied here and there. And yet it is He!

Chapter Nineteen

It Remains Tough

But then daily life is by no means just easy smooth-running times. It is constantly disturbed by small things or big. Something lost, something gone wrong, responsibilities to fulfil, demanding children, finances, sickness, clashes of personalities, differences of viewpoint, decisions to be made. And at these many moments, self doesn't remain spontaneous! It comes very much alive and we have our human reactions. It is at this spot that we find it hard to grasp that this is precisely God's purpose that His sons should be involved in disturbing human situations. The positive must have its negative to manifest through, so we must learn to the full what it is to be a negative. It was said of Jesus Himself that though He was a Son, He yet learned obedience through the things which He suffered, and thus knew that the Son could do nothing of Himself. We ask a useless question and mistake the meaning of life if we say, 'Will there be no let-up from continual pressures?' No. Let me face this in the full depth of its implications. If I am to function in my proper place as a son and inheritor of God's universe in my eternal destiny, I need to learn first how a son functions in adverse circumstances. A swimmer grows strong against the tide, not with it. So my privilege is to feel the impacts on my negative humanity of all that can disturb me. It is tribulation, Paul said, which works in me finding and experiencing the God of deliverances. It is the trial of my faith which works maturity in me, says James. There is a fundamental principle here, and when we see that, we can expect and welcome what the world calls problems and frustrations. If in our future destiny we are to be at ease in letting God through in friendly areas of responsibility, it can only be because we gradually became experienced in letting Him through in the enemy's territory. So these years in the world against the tide are no mistake. They are not something which need not have been. They have to be. If we suffer with Him, we shall reign with Him. We must first learn therefore, and accept with praise as the adventure of adversity, the reality of life's pressures and our constant negative human reactions to them. By this means only, first finding how earthen our vessels are, shall we then by stages be ever quicker, as Jesus so wonderfully was, in knowing how to replace our negative with His positive. That way we become at home in the eternal fact that His strength can only be made perfect in our weakness; and find Paul's secret that 'when I am weak, then am I strong'. This is of vast importance because we so mistakenly have got used to thinking that we are wrong when we have these negative reactions. No, they must be.

So we shall always start by feeling human hurts, fears, dislikes, unwillingness, coldness, powerlessness, lusts, angers, jealousies, and all the list of them. Start, we say, because the start of such reactions is not sin. A human must be human, and Jesus himself had to feel temptation to be tempted in all points. Sin is not in the start, but in the continuance. Negative reactions are not sin. They are the negative stirrings which are the jumping off point for faith. Sins are when, instead of taking those jumps of faith, we continue in the reaction. 'When lust hath conceived, it bringeth forth sin.' When we 'marry' the self-reaction, accept and continue in it, then the child is sin. We have already quoted how Paul went as far as to 'take pleasure' in those experiences which hurt us humans: what he named as feeling his weakness, being hurt or insulted by others, having personal needs, being persecuted, having insoluble problems: 'for', he said, 'when I am weak, then am I strong'. Note, not 'then I shall be made strong or become strong or seek for strength'. No, 'then am I strong', because all he had to do was to recognize who he really was, Christ in him. So to have negative human reactions is not sin, but our opportunities for faith. Sin is when we continue in the reaction, as we all do at times, and then act out some form of 'the works of the flesh'.

It is this balanced understanding of our daily living which will save us from false condemnation. We shall not say we were all wrong because we felt so and so – a very ordinary day, no great victories or guidances, no particular elevated feelings, the pressures of daily events, the children's problems and the work conditions, attacks of depression, no answers to situations. 'Surely I should have been brighter or more effective or a better witness. Haven't I missed opportunities and not been courageous enough?' And so the self-searching tears us down. Cut it out! Praise the Lord. Recognize that if you have a sin, it is the sin of unbelief in doubting or questioning whether He was being Himself in you despite feelings or appearances. Believe and praise!

And where these have been conscious sins, or we feel they may have been sins, it is here John tells us that there is daily cleansing in our daily walk. The Epistles constantly use the word 'walk', and that points us to step by step, because that is the only way a person can walk. So when in our walk, we feel we have missed the mark, even if we are not sure whether it is over the line into a committed sin, or just one of these attitudes, the way out is simple: admission to ourselves and that is of course inwardly to God; bold recognition that all the sins of all the world ceased to exist in God's sight (and therefore in ours) by the shedding of the Blood of Christ two thousand years ago: the word of faith which we say within ourselves that therefore that sin exists no more: praise in having the cleansed conscience: then walking on as if the thing never happened. Quick sinning. Quick cleansing.

Chapter Twenty

The Key to Everything

If this gives us some basis for normal Christian living, we shall now move on to the heart of things which we can call the key to everything. We have now come full circle to where we started. We said at the beginning that our total revolution is our return from being matter-people to what we really are – spirit-people. And the extent of that revolution is beyond all words, and reaches right down to the tiniest detail or the greatest mountain in our lives. We took a brief glance at the raw fact that either the Bible is an unreliable record, or the men of God from earliest years to the final happenings listed in Hebrews 11, lived in a dimension right in the middle of this earthly world, in which things took place which cannot be accounted for by human reason. Having already referred to a number from Old Testament records, we need only look at the life of Jesus, who the Bible makes plain in Hebrews 2 became wholly one of us, a true human. It is plain that He did not see earth events as we see them. He did not look *at* them but *through* them – to what? To the reality of which they were only external distorted shadow forms. He did not look away elsewhere to call His Father on to the scene. He saw Him already always there at the hidden heart of the apparent condition of need. He saw the One of whom it is said, 'Who is above all, and through all, and in you all,' and, 'by Him all things consist'. The distortions had their origin in our fallen human believings, which in their grab and grasp, had brought need, disease, and disharmony into God's perfect world, so that we have to live life out in a world of thorns and thistles by the sweat of our brows.

So how did Jesus act? In the coolest possible manner He continually saw right through the lack or disease. Did they fish all night and catch nothing? He held no prayer meeting, but just said, 'Launch out and let down your nets for a draught ... and they inclosed a great multitude of fishes.' They were on the lake when a big storm arose and the boat was filling with water. When they called out to Him and woke Him from sleep, He actually rebuked them for being afraid they would drown. Have we any better faith today?! Don't we still see *at* storms and fear them? And all He did was to see *through* the storm to the Father of all weather and all calm, who is at the heart of the storm because everything is a form of Him, and spoke that word of faith, 'Peace, be still'. We see diseases and death. He evidently did not. You don't tell a man with a withered hand to stretch it out, if you see it's withered. It is only if you see through to a whole hand with God's life in that man, that you could tell him to do such a thing. He actually only saw sleep when we see death. He said of Jairus' daughter, 'She is not dead, but sleepeth.' And they laughed Him to scorn! Who wouldn't! They bring Him five loaves to feed five thousand. No concern, no going aside to pray, just an order to get the people settled down in rows of fifty. Meanwhile he 'lifted His eyes to heaven' (it was necessary that they all see the source of power to be beyond Himself), blessed, brake and 'they were all filled'. And so water was turned to wine, money came out of a fish's mouth, and all the healings of blind, leprous, deaf, dumb. And Peter picked up this way of faith and boldly asked to walk on the water, and walked. Evidently Jesus took no account of the laws of gravity! And Peter followed through after Pentecost and said to the lame man by the gate of the Temple, 'Silver and gold have I none, but such as I have, give I thee. In the name of Jesus Christ of Nazareth, rise up and walk.' Such as he, Peter, had – not God! You see what I am saying? I am not saying, 'Imitate Him.' Faith is not imitation, but action each on our level.

But I am delving into this key fact, that God is not limited to laborius matter-means of production based on human reasoning. It is the Fall which bound us down to human thinking; and Jesus said we are not to live by 'taking thought'. God is spirit, matter is only a condensed form of spirit, and we have tied ourselves down in our race-outlook to matter, and matter being the reality. But in Christ, by union with Him in His death and resurrection, and by His Spirit joined to our spirits, we are no longer matter-people, but spirit-people. 'Ye are not in the flesh, but in the Spirit, if so be that the Spirit of God dwell in you.'

Now that means a totally different outlook on every detail of life, small or great, insofar as I recognize the falseness of my natural outlook and practise the habit of changing it. That is why we say it is the key to everything – everything. Nothing is outside its reach. It does not make us less practical or sensible, but quietly seeing and approaching everything from a new dimension, or rather as being in that new dimension. It is also wholly logical if it is true, as I believe and there is all this Bible evidence that it is.

Say a thing is just some small household or business problem, or some major world situation. I start by the way I am looking at it, for this is our whole first point, that we are inner people and are controlled by the way we inwardly see a thing, in other words by our believing. Now I always am meant, as a practical human, to start seeing it as it outwardly appears. I have mislaid something. There is a financial need. There is a relationship problem. There is sickness or tragedy. Of course I begin by believing it as it appears to be. That means I am bound by a sense of helplessness, or a drive to try somehow to clear it; but my spirit is clouded by my negative outlook; or of course in a thousand things it never even occurs to me that there could be another way of looking at it. What is more, I am confirming and strengthening the condition that is bothering me by my attitude of believing in it as it is. This is our whole realm of outlook on all life, and any other outlook is merely phony.

But now, supposing the real truth is that this outward situation is only an outward appearance. Really only a shadow. Suppose the real fact is that, as there is only God in the universe, this situation is God in disguise. It is He in some outer clothing of need, tragedy, problem. They are the distortions of God's perfect world, but they are only distortions. God's perfection is the only reality, and, as He did by Jesus, by the authority of the faith of His believing sons, He manifests Himself today in His perfection through the outer appearances of imperfection. This Paul says has always been His own planned purpose for the world (Romans 8:19–21) –

through His sons to complete the replacement of its present 'bondage of corruption' by 'glorious liberty'; and this we sons can do today in our local situations, as Jesus our elder brother did.

So we are daringly saying that wherever there is a need, small or great, wherever there is a disturbed or tragic situation, God is not just looking on and to be called upon to intervene. No, God is the Real One right in the situation, and it is only His distorted clothing; and we preserve the clothing by believing it to be the real.

Now in utmost simplicity, without changing an outward thing, let us transfer our believings. That's all. Let us deliberately affirm, against all appearance, that this is not the difficulty it appears to be. Instead of looking at the situation, let us look through – to God, again not afar off, but the very situation being He in disguise. He with supply, He with solution, He with change, where we only see the opposite.

Chapter Twenty-one

God Determines, Not Permits

Then let us take it further. Let us specifically believe that He is coming through and will manifest Himself. Let it be specific so that it is an inner word of faith; and the best way such an inner word takes outer form is by praise. All we have now done is to transfer our believing from the negative to Him the Positive, and it is our believing which lets Him through. Our believing doesn't do a thing in itself. God is the doer. God is the one who deliberately put us in this problem situation and thus awakens us to get into faith action. And the faith action is my responsibility as a son of God, invested with authority to be the one by whose word of faith He reveals Himself in some concrete form. He is already there. The supply is there for He is the supply, where our human eyes see only the need. We merely, by our word of faith, affirm His fulfilling presence. Just as at the beginning the Word said, 'Let there be light, and there was light.'

Now let us backtrack and go into this in more detail, just because it is so revolutionary and universal in its application.

First, there is our necessary basis of seeing God in everything and everybody. We won't go back again over what we sought to show at the beginning that the universe is God manifesting Himself, Spirit slowed down to the point of visibility. We either 'see through' to that wonderful fact, or we don't. If we don't, there is not much point in following through along the lines in which Jesus evidently 'saw through' to His Father, the hidden presence in the apparent conditions of material need, disease, or death. But, if we do, then that which needs strong confirmation, if we are to be strong in faith under any conditions, is the certainty that God doesn't sit by and 'permit' various adverse or tragic situations; but He actually 'determines' them.

There are a series of very plain evidences of this in Bible incidents, and I don't think they can be bettered, though so well known. The most obvious and complete is that Jesus, when approaching His death, did not look at it as a machination of the devil, except in the sense that the devil was God's agent. He admitted that this was 'the prince of this world coming' to assault him, but He added 'he hath nothing in Me': in other words, Satan could not touch Him in His real inner self on the level of His inner believings, and could only attack his outer body. Then He said later, when they came to arrest Him, 'The cup which my Father hath given Me, shall I not drink it?' That was final. This was not the devil, but His own Father responsible for this. That is perfect. Then Peter confirms it so completely in his Pentecost talk, the first official pronouncement at the birth of the church. 'You crucified Him with your wicked hands, but you were doing what was God's determined counsel and foreknowledge.' No mere permissiveness about that. And in the first recorded prayer of the early church, they said, 'Of a truth against Thy holy child

Jesus, both Herod and Pontius Pilate, with the gentiles, and the people of Israel, were gathered together, for to do whatsoever Thy hand and Thy counsel determined before to be done.' Surely conclusive!

The other famous saying was when, after Joseph had been sold as a slave by his brothers, and imprisoned through Potiphar's wife, and had fourteen years of bondage and confinement, but was then elevated by Pharaoh to be his chief minister, and was thus able to rescue his brethren from famine, he said, 'You thought evil unto me, but God meant it for good ... God did send me before you to preserve life.' Conclusive again. And add to that, many passing statements such as that the Assyrians were 'the rod of Mine anger'; and Nebuchadnezzar, come to destroy Jerusalem, was 'Nebuchadnezzar My servant.' And the various swarms of locusts, caterpillars and others which reduced Israel to famine, were, the Lord said through Joel, 'My great army which I sent among you.' And the Lord sent a lying spirit to deceive Ahab. And it was God who stirred up Satan to assault Job, not Satan who persuaded God.

This gives me boldness and authority to say what would seem to the outward eye to be clearly contrary to the character of God as love, that whatever befalls me, or whatever apparent horrors are happening in the world, God sent those, God determined that – not just permitted them. And I think we see the explanation clearly enough when we have got it clear that outer sufferings are not the real suffering, but inner sorrow is – in other words, the way we take a thing.

We saw in the account of the Fall that suffering was to be humanity's greatest blessing. Even before there was a human race, we are told in Hebrews 2:10 that the only way the Father could have a matured, perfected family of sons could be by His own Son, their Creator, becoming perfected as Leader-Saviour and Elder Brother by sufferings. Why? Because only by opposites can a thing be known in its reality: only by a full experience of the wrong way can we be established in the right.

So sufferings cry out to us that something is dreadfully wrong with our condition, and compel us to find our release from them, and from the inner sorrow which is their effect on us. In our blindness, which attributes the suffering to the outward conditions which appear to make us suffer, we seek to escape by altering the outward conditions. But at last, by His merciful pressures on us by suffering, the Father compels us to face up to the truth: that our true sufferings are within and not without. They are because we are inwardly committing the one fundamental sin of 'the evil heart of unbelief'. We know in our inner beings whose offspring we are, but we refuse to bend our stiff necks and inwardly acknowledge that our true suffering is our rebellious, resenting, resisting inner attitude. We refuse to acknowledge Him in our suffering situations, and accept Him in His love, in place of questioning how He can be responsible for what is happening to us. And we escape it still further by looking at the sufferings of others and asking how God can be responsible for that, not yet knowing in ourselves that all sufferings are purposed as redemptive in the individual lives of each sufferer; and the only true suffer is the perpetrator, unless it brings him also to repentance.

But thank God we can come to this final point of

reversing our antagonism, only because He first revealed Himself to us in outward form by His forgiving and restoring love in His Son, who has suffered with and for us. When at last we do that, and transfer our believings from our outward suffering conditions and our consequent resistance to them and our defiance of Himself in them, and believe in Him and His word of grace with no strings of questioning attached, then we have found the key and turned it in the lock: our real suffering was our inner unbelief.

We now see through to Him alone who purposed these outer sufferings to establish us – the only way to do so. We now recognize by faith that it is He coming through in some new perfect manifestation of Himself in love and power. The sufferings are only the outer shadow cast by our unbelief. Then we praise and rejoice, the joy of birth swallows up the pangs of travail; and we begin to practise the fundamental principle of no longer seeing anything as evil to us, or a problem, or a frustration. We don't 'see' those things. There are no prison bars left, for there is no outer prison to this eye of faith which sees only the Father in perfection in all things. For whatever the outer situation, in our inner selves we can always believe and praise that this is God's perfection for ourselves; and then our outer prison conditions are found to be open doors to share the same secret with the many others around us in their desperate sorrows, because they have got these outer sufferings and outer bondages questions as confused as we had. We are free – free to love – and he that loves has God dwelling in him and His love perfected in him. The whole question of suffering, its meaning and values, is largely the theme of Peter's first letter.

So now we have the grounds for the change from negative to positive believing which has to take place in every incident small or large. It is as revolutionary as we have eyes to see it. Everything in our lives is as we see it in the outer form – every material thing, every person, every happening. We are believing what our eyes see. That is the only way we know how to live as common sense people, and we call that reality. But what if it isn't? If it is only an outer material form, just as my body is my outer form; and reality is spirit, God manifested through forms?

Now if I begin to be absurd enough to practise the habit of seeing everything and everybody and every happening in that dimension, how do I act? First, I act perfectly normally in relation to everything and everybody. I get on with living. But then all sorts of things happen that I would like to see different – again both things and people. Well, some changes or supplies are within my reach, I can handle them. Very well, I do. But some are not. Now I am reaching nearer the bone. It is here that I am getting my practice in acting as a son of God, a spirit-person, not a matter-person. I look right through that situation, practical need, or whatever, and I say, 'That is only appearance. That is real on the matter world level, but I'm not really living there.' In my real self, my inner spirit joined to God's Spirit, that need is not real to me. It is not there to me. I only see my God of all supply where my natural eyes see only the lack.

That is how we 'die' to the natural outlook. We are seeing through. If it was God who put us in this place of need, then that is only the reverse side of His coin, and we don't live on the reverse side, and don't see it. The other side is the supply already there, for He is always all fullness. So now by the 'renewing of our minds', we are beginning to see clearly. He meant us to have the problem to have practice in not seeing the problem but only Himself at the inner centre. So we now transfer our believing from natural seeing to seeing in the Spirit. We are now believing Him, and the problem (to us unreal) only His outer clothing.

Chapter Twenty-two

The Word of Faith

And now for the word of faith. We have said all along
that a person functions as a person by the decisive
moments when we move from general thinking to
specific choice, and that is what the Bible calls 'the word
of faith'. We say, not ask or hope. We 'say unto this
mountain (which is our present problem) be thou removed and be thou cast into the sea'. We speak our
word of faith, 'God, you are doing so and so. Thank
You.'

But wait a minute. The snag always is, 'Yes, but what
right have I to say God will do that thing, just because I
want or need it?' The reason we ask that is because we
still have so much on us of the old grave clothes of sus-
picion of our self-loving selves. We doubt our motives.
We wonder whether in daring to say God will do so and
so, maybe some trivial thing, we are not presumptuous,
kind of tempting God. But that is because we haven't
yet settled into our new union relationship, or forgotten
it for a moment. We ARE one. Therefore I freely take it
that my desires are His desires in me. That is precisely
what Jesus Himself said to us, 'Whatsoever ye desire,
when ye pray, believe . . .' He saw us as we are in the
union in Him, and therefore that now our normal living

and wishes are His. And what He is eagerly watching for is our new-found boldness. That is why the centurion thrilled Him who sent and said, 'You needn't come to my house to heal my servant. I am not worthy. Just speak the word'; and that was when Jesus exclaimed, 'I have not found so great faith, no, not in Israel', and was refreshed by the vision of the coming millions of believing gentiles in the kingdom. And when that Syrophenician woman threw His word back at Him, when He had said that He couldn't give the children's bread to the dogs, and she countered, 'Yes, but the dogs eat the crumbs!' Great to get one over Jesus, and wasn't He delighted. He had just made that tough remark to spark this counter-attack in her! And His own parable of the importunate friend getting bread from his unwilling friend at midnight, and knocking till he got it, and Jesus' comment that he got it because of his 'importunity' (Greek – shamelessness, nerve, cheek). So what is needed by us is to take those plunges, simply on the basis of our desires in a situation, and say the word. That word releases the Spirit through us as sons, each handling our own local affairs, to bring in to substantial form the thing we have spoken for.

Once we have said that word, that's it. It is no longer our affair. It was God all the way through getting some perfect purpose of His into visibility; but He operates through His sons exercising their prerogatives of free decision. Now God has taken on. It is not for us to make a mockery of our word of faith by repeating it, or still less by slipping back into asking. No, we can thank many times that He has done something; we practice the habit of seeing the thing as done with the eye of faith. But that's all. Above all we must not look around now to see how it happens, or if there is a delay, ask why. That is not our business, and it is as good as calling into question the honesty of our believing and His faithfulness. If we are in a tight spot, we don't see it with the eye of negative believing, as a tight place, we still continue to call the things that be not as though they were – yes, even if we die not having received the promises!

And does this include believing for people as well as things? Most certainly, and really most important of all. But again, for me, that has meant a revolutionary stretching of my understanding of God. Since I have seen what Paul said of the whole human race that 'in Him we live and move and have our being', and thus by no means is He 'far from any one of us', I see Him at the hidden centre of every person as well as every situation. I see that in Jesus' speaking of all men as 'prodigal sons', or 'lost sheep'. It gives me a different attitude to everybody. I have been so accustomed to seeing people negatively (except myself!!), and starting by looking at a person as likely a non-believer rather than a believer. I see the prodigal part of people rather than the son. But that parable conveys to me the father eagerly watching down the road for the wandering son, which means he was expecting that he would come to his senses when he had had enough of the husks, and there he was running out to welcome him. And when the other prodigal, the elder brother, was shewing his serpent-self-nature (which we all have) in his jealousy and self-love (expressed in self-righteousness), all that beautiful father did was not to give him a word of rebuke, anymore than he did to the wandering prodigal, but calling him a son and reminding him that all was already his. I am sure that this bout of jealousy was just another swine's husks experience in the form which could reach the elder brother; and what broke him was not some negative rebuke looking at him as an unpleasant self-seeker, but that word of love which could open his eyes by contrast to his selfish self. Those are the father's ways. He just sees humans as precious sons misusing themselves, deceived into believing that they can find themselves in other ways; but wait a bit, they will have had enough of the wrong ways and be ready to return.

I do not say that, having lost our sonship through the Fall, it is not possible for us never to regain it, but choose to remain children of the devil. The Bible makes plain there are such, and that there is the outer darkness, the worm that dieth not, and the fire not quenched. But I take it that when God chooses to put me in a certain human family and links me in life with certain people, then as a son, I use my authority to declare in faith their return to God; and then to see them, not as they still are in rebellious unbelief, but with the eye of faith as sons back in the family. I see people as lost sons rather than the devil's children, in whom the Spirit is busy calling them back home. It gives me love, understanding and faith rather than condemnation.

Chapter Twenty-three

How Do I Look At People

But a lesson I am very slow to learn is how to see every individual in the world as they really are. Here are a company of people acting together in a certain cause, an industrial union, a political party, a crowd of demonstrators; or on a larger scale, adherents of a certain religion or members of an ethnic group: and my normal reaction is to view them in the mass, and, if I don't like who they are or what they stand for, judge them negatively in the mass, and have an antagonistic feeling towards them.

But more than that, I find that my general attitude to individuals whom I pass in the street, sit with in a conveyance, see pictured in a paper or TV, is equally negative. My first general reactions are critical and to dislike them; and this specially so, if I know something about them which justifies my attitude, a condemned criminal, the perpetrator of a horrible deed, an enemy in a conflict; or much closer to home, my own neighbours or workmates or club members. The very way folk dress or look or speak has that same effect on me.

That is not difficult to understand because the hard facts of life, our hurts, our let-downs, our own home conflicts and broken relationships, our unjust treatment in business or society, and all the cruelties of life which stream in on us from the news media, build a suspicious attitude in us. Also subtly we project our own former dislike of ourselves and fear of others on to other people.

But now apply the same principle of positive faith towards every man. Let me see every man as he really is: a human spirit who has his being in God, but like the rest of us, has been caught up in seeking to find himself in the mistaken ways of self-fulfilment apart from God. So every man is a deluded self, but in his delusion is quite certain that he is on a right track. We all live by faith – the faith that we are right – even if that is against the laws of God and man. A burglar is right, a murderer is right, the enemy is right, the sex-obsessed is right, up to the 'highest' delusion, which Jesus spoke of, 'Whosoever killeth you will think he doeth God service': and Solomon put it in one phrase: 'There is a way that seemeth right unto a man, but the end thereof are the ways of death.'

But now supposing we practise the habit of seeing others as we see ourselves. We thought we were right, and trying to find the right way the best we knew how. We have had our eyes opened, by the Spirit of truth working on us till we did at last respond, and now we are sure we are right – in the Father, Son and Spirit. But that certainly makes us understanding of all men everywhere, who are equally somewhere along the road of following some conviction that this is the way of self-fulfilment for them; and if they are on the wrong road, we are equally sure that the Spirit of love and truth, that Hound of Heaven, 'follows, follows after' them too, until, as Francis Thompson (who had himself been a

drug addict), so marvellously put it, that Voice echoes
in the blinded heart: 'All things betray thee who be-
trayest Me: naught shelters thee who will not shelter
Me: naught contentest thee who conten'st not Me: all
things I took from thee I did but take, not for thy harms,
but just that thou might'st seek it in my arms: all that
thy child's mistake fancies as lost, I have stored for thee
at home, rise, clasp My hand and come!'

I think this was Paul's attitude, when he did not side-
step sin, speaking of those who 'being past feeling have
given themselves over to work all uncleanness with
greediness'; but he had first said of them with true
depth of penetration into the misguided human spirit,
that they were those who walked in mental vanity, with
darkened understanding, and ignorance of the life
of God, through blindness of heart (Ephesians
4:17–19). He recognized that their sinful life was their
present heart's love and choice, but that its effects
were a vast blindness and ignorance: and he had compassion on the blindness more than condemnation of the
sin.

Paul had said the same, as we have seen, to the
Athenian who was not satisfied with crude idolatory with
its graven images, and had erected this altar to the
Unknown God. Paul did not just see a member of a
'heathen' people, but a seeking human spirit whose
being is in God, but is ignorant of Him whom he seeks:
'whom ye ignorantly worship (and the "ye" implies that
Paul counted on there being more than one!), Him declare I unto you', and 'the times of this ignorance God
winked at'.

And what more perfect and final in the right ways of
seeing fellow-humans than the Saviour's own words on

the cross: 'Father, forgive them for they know not what they do'? He looked through brutal cruelty or careless indifference to precious humans in ignorance, and doing what they thought to be right, and that is what the Father's forgiveness is for.

Now I apply that to my daily reactions to people. I must not keep my believing, as I have done for so long, on outward appearances. I must not lump together all the people involved in some combined action I disapprove of (and my disapproval of the action may be largely because I don't understand) as just a crowd of prejudiced of self-seeking people: but I must see them as individuals, in each of whose hearts God is working as He is in mine. Equally I must not look with a jaundiced eye on individual outward behaviour or appearance of which I don't approve. I must practice this same principle of transferred believing, transferred to who each person really is – a created and loved human in the being of God, really therefore a form of God, a human expression of God, gone wrong, – that he may be made right: and God in His Spirit of love is as busy working in him, disturbing his false beliefs, as He has been on me through the years. Then I love my neighbour as myself. Just as I always find tolerance for myself, so I can for my neighbour. In fact, I must get this habit, of which my African friends always spoke, of realizing that when I point one finger at my neighbour, the other three fingers are pointing back at me! Follow them first! And I must be sensitized to my real sin, which is believing flesh rather than spirit, believing in what I outwardly dislike in my neighbour instead of believing and seeing him as one in God's own being, in whose inner centre God is continually working in mercy. And I shall build my neighbour by faith and love, instead of destroying him by believing evil.

Paul remarkably stretches this depth of insight into every person who has not had the chance of contact with God's outwardly codified laws. In Romans 2:5–16, he is confronting his Jewish brethen who had the law but did not keep it, and he says that God judges every individual not by his outer profession, but his inner sincerity of heart and the life lived in conformity to it. He boldly says God 'will render to every man according to his deeds'; whether his purpose in life has been to live rightly and sought to do so, or to live wrongly and intended to do so. Then he analyses what goes on within a person who has never had the outward law as given to Israel, yet is living by the standards of the law, and doing it 'naturally'. 'How can that be?' – asks Paul. Because he accepts the control of an inner law, which really all men have if they will conform to it: and this man does accept that inner law in his heart, which means he chooses to do so and wants to do so. The consequences, Paul says, are that his own conscience (the echo of the Spirit in him) confirms to him that he is right, and on the mind level he is continually checking himself up as to whether this action would be right or wrong: and then Paul ends by saying that on the day when he and all men stand before God the Judge of all, God's standard of judgement will be, not on the externals, but on what went on in the heart of each, 'the secrets of men', and that He will judge those 'by Jesus Christ'.

Peter saw a flash of the same when, on arriving at the house of the gentile Cornelius, he exclaimed, 'Of a truth I perceive that God is no respecter of persons: but in every nation he that feareth God and worketh righteousness is accepted with Him.' And when Paul spoke of the need of the gospel being preached to all men, he added twice over (in Romans 10:18 and Colossians 1:23), 'But I say, Have they not heard? Yes verily, their sound went into all the earth, and their words unto the end of the world'; and called it 'the gospel which was preached to every creature which is under heaven'.

In Romans 1:18–20, Paul then reveals that there is within all men an inner knowledge that there is a living God whom they can worship, confirmed outwardly to them by the visible creation; and so all are without excuse if they have not worshipped Him – which means that pagans can worship Him!

But without Christ, our human forms of worship cannot deliver us from our fallen selves. There are a large number of religions in the world today. Each, if we look into it, has a strand of truth, but the rope is Satan's. The Moslems proclaim the uniqueness of God: the Hindus that God is the immanent presence in all things: the Buddhists that the human race is ensnared by its self-desires and deliverance is freedom from self: the Animists that there is a spirit world: even the Humanists and Marxists that we humans should be a brotherhood. But can these save a man from his sins and self-centredness? No. Because we are the captives of the god of self-centredness, our very religions can only build up our own self-image: *my* religion, *my* code, of ethics, *my* special God; and we turn them at their highest into means of improving and purifying the self, which as we have seen, is an impossibility, for we still remain self-centred selves: or, what is their main effect on the multitudes of their followers, to debase them, as Paul said in Romans 1, into all forms of demonism and idolatry, into horrible caricatures of the living God, and into licensed deification of human lust. Thus, the devil uses religion by the fanatical loyalty of its adherents into his final bastion of preserving his slaves in the kingdom of darkness. And he just as cleverly uses the religion of Christianity for the same purpose! (We can understand Bonhoeffer's call for a 'Religionless Christianity'!) That is why we must take the gospel to every creature, for only God's Son, come in human flesh can, by his death and resurrection, lift those humans who receive Him out of their self-centred bondages. Only He can bring them into true selfhood, which is not I living, but Christ living in me. He only is the Way, Truth and Life which brings us back to the Father.

And yet, and yet, we see by what Paul and Peter said, the quenchless Spirit of God at work in every human being who has ever been on this earth, through that witnessing conscience, through the law written in the heart, through the glory of the visible creation, through man's own condemning or approving thoughts; and there appear to be those, not for us to say how many, who did conform their, what we call pagan, hearts to God's law as they understood Him, and they stand before a judge of mercy in Jesus Christ. Let us at least look on those we call 'non-Christians', as ones who are inwardly being worked upon by the Father whose offspring we all are. I even love the searchings of that great mixed pagan mind in Robert Browning's poem, *Caliban upon Setebos*.

And speaking of judgement, it must rightly be first a terror to all of us human law-breakers. 'The fear of the

Lord is the beginning of wisdom', but as we progress from fear to finding our loving acceptance, do we not need to change our view of judgement? We are often told that we should look with fearfulness, even though we are Christ's, at His coming Judgement Seat for the believers. But should we? If He is only love, then if He has some judgement to pass on me when I am before Him, won't I recognize the total rightness of it, that it was only love speaking what it always must – the truth? And what is more, if I am told, as I am, that I shall be like Him when I see Him as He is, and know as I am known when 'face to face', and that I am predestined to be conformed to His image, can't I therefore take it that any touch of judgement that day, any burnings of wood, hay and stubble, will only be to conform me to His likeness? So I eagerly anticipate the blessing of being judged! And anyhow Paul said that when that Day does come, it won't be loads of disapproval to weigh us down, but 'then shall every man have praise of God'! (1 Corinthians 4:5).

Chapter Twenty-four

What About World Situations?

If that is true of my attitudes to individuals, it also makes all the difference in my attitudes to my fellow humans in the mass, in all our various subdivisions: races, nations, governments: or in our more regional groupings into organizations of every persuasion, companies, unions, societies, political parties.

I find my normal reactions to be negatively critical, suspicious, and tending to see the worst in them. Now is this my right attitude? We know that most are plainly geared to the one end of making the best of this fallen world for our own self-interests. A few may seek to give God His place in their affairs: the majority are materialistic, self-centred, or even aggressively atheistic. That does not mean that there are not believing Christians in their ranks where there is freedom of religious faith. There are those who have a special calling to bring all they can of God and the gospel into human society and participate in political or social organizations. Thank God there are such; but we know it can only be patchwork in a world which still 'lieth in the wicked one'. We know that the only ultimate restoration is in the personal return of our Lord Jesus Christ and in 'the new heavens and new earth wherein dwelleth righteousness'. But whether personally involved or not, how am I to view or be related to human organizations on the local, national or international level?

Now how does God look on the affairs of nations? The prophet Habbakuk, in an agony over the horror of the godless Assyrians being God's cruel scourge on backsliding Israel, came through to a glorious vision. He saw not only the inevitable judgement there must be on all sin, but also a greater fact: that God 'is of purer eyes than to behold evil'. As a consequence he had the tremendous revelation, quoted three times over in the New Testament, that 'the just shall live by his faith', by seeing through to how God sees it all and what He is doing. But what does it mean that God is of purer eyes than to behold evil, and that the pure in heart see God, and to the pure all things are pure?

We know, by the message of the whole Bible and especially the Old Testament prophets, that there must be the wrath and judgement of God on evil. God could be God in no other way. The opposite to God must have its opposite effects of corruption, the curse and hell. 'God is angry with the wicked every day', angry for their sakes, both for what they do to others and to themselves. So all history bears witness to God's judgement on all nations, for all are infected with the virus of evil. God does bless and prosper in measure where there is evidence of some of 'the righteousness which exalteth a nation'. He has preserved some order and freedom in the world by law-abiding, and sometimes to some extent God-fearing nations. He preserved some freedom in the world through the British Empire, despite its gross exploitation of the weaker, which had now come under rightful judgement; and He is doing the same today through the United States, which does show some care and concern for freedom and for helping the less privileged. Yet Reinhold Niebuhr was right as a modern prophet who persisted in his message that all nations and governments are under judgement, and the ultimate hope is only in the return of Christ.

But if this is true, as we know it is, is there not another way in which we can view God's judgements? Paul said it in Romans 11:32, that God has shut all up in unbelief, which means that He meant us to swallow our bitter pill. But why? To judge, condemn, destroy? No, 'that He might have mercy on all'. Beautiful statement! So Habbakuk's 'Thou art of purer eyes than to behold evil' can be interpreted as meaning that God sees *through*. He does not see evil just as evil with all its consequences. He sees His misguided human family learning vital lessons by their mishandling of themselves, and by these means (which is another way of saying participating in the wrath of God), being pressed into the search for the release to be only found in Christ. So God does not 'see evil' as something ultimately destructive, but redemptive. He 'sees' it only as the reverse side of those opposites we have talked about, which, when put back where it belongs, disappears, as poison is swallowed up by its antidote, sickness by health, etc. It isn't ultimately real. Only the positive has ultimate and eternal reality (though by their free choice, the Bible makes plain, men can remain eternally in the negative of hell).

So we do the same. We see menacing powers like communism, or brutally authoritarian governments, or dishonest and greedy business firms, or unjustified labour strikes (though there have been many justified ones), or attempts to outlaw religion, or the blatant contempt for moral standards and the new permissive society, we see all as God's purposed ways of bringing humanity to an end of itself. We praise God for each. While God is not responsible for man going his rebellious ways, He has it all in hand to issue in 'the good pleasure of His goodness', so we praise Him. Glory to God! He that sitteth in the heavens laughs, so we laugh too! We can never do that if we see evil with the normal human outlook; but we can and do when instead of seeing the evil, we see God in His perfection, and there has never been anything but perfection to the single eye which sees only Him in everything.

For long some of us have said, 'Don't be all stirred up about communism.' It is God's appointment just as much as the Assyrians were the rod of His anger, or Nebuchadnezzar His servant. Praise Him, and watch. And haven't we seen under the banner of atheistic materialism the farce of a supposed brotherhood of man by brutal suppression of freedom? For while it has claimed to condemn our admitted bourgeois selfishness, it could only replace it by its own form of proletarian selfishness, imposed by force. Fallen self cannot change self. And what has it resulted in as a reaction? A tremendous upsurge of renewed faith, a great wave of spiritual revival, the most widespread in the history of the church. And the same through the drug and free-sex obsessions which have so captured youth. Never before in history has there been a youth-led uprising of Jesus people, so that the Name which was held in contempt or as a curse word is held high in honour by thousands of youth today.

So we are taking an uncompromising line which

covers any possible world event, however deeply disturbing or frightening – wars, revolutions, political dictatorships, or internal upsets in the national economy, or what often weigh more heavily on us – forebodings for the future. In face of the worst of which we can conceive or is already happening, we turn our face away from its frightening appearance and we say, 'That is not what is real to us.' What we see is God only, always determining what appears like evil for new resurrections, and He already has the resurrection which will appear in due time, and we laugh that laugh of faith!

Thank God, we know that 'in all our afflictions He is afflicted', and it is through Jesus that the world has learned compassion. Hospitals, homes for the aged, food for the starving, child care, the missionary ministry of healing and education in backward countries, are only a few of the ways by which the love which flowed from the Incarnation and Calvary has widened to a great river. These are also like lights in the dark places of human affairs: but we all await the only Great Light – the coming of the Lord, when at last the heart of God will be satisfied, and ours also, in swords being beaten into ploughshares, the wolf lying down with the lamb, and the earth filled with the knowledge of the Lord like the waters cover the sea.

And we do the same with those kind of news shocks we get daily as they touch us on the raw through the radio and newspapers, and which put a load on our spirits: the floods and earthquakes, the road accidents, the murders, muggings and robberies, the crowded jails, the stream of human tragedy. How can we praise God in these and for these?

But while our hearts are torn by tragedy and

sufferings, and our hands will help where they can, we still see through and praise, even though we appear heartless in doing so; for we dare to see love's purpose to every incident, and with the eye of faith, God meaning for good what man has meant for evil; therefore we do not see the evil, and even increase it by our believing in it; we refuse to see it as evil. We take every opportunity not only to minister to suffering bodies, but to share with the bitter hearts, (which is the true suffering) the only true balm, the assurance of God's love and His perfect ways. And if we cannot share it, we can and do boldly praise God here and now for what seems nothing but horror, and so contribute our share in the Spirit by at least ourselves exchanging the garment of praise for the spirit of heaviness.

Chapter Twenty-five

Health and Healing

Then there is the health and healing question. It is plain that all who came to Jesus were healed. But not so today. Let us face it. Even with those who have the best known public healing meetings, only a small proportion go away healed, and many hundreds unhealed. Yet there is healing. The Bible makes that plain. There are the two extremes among Christians – those who speak of healing as if it is the normal thing to expect and something is wrong with our faith if it does not happen; and those who really don't believe in it for today, though to cover themselves, they may say, 'Of course God can heal'.

It is true that Jesus had that perfect relationship with His Father, by which without a hesitation He spoke the words or gave the touch which healed every kind of disease, and all who came to Him in faith were healed; and it is true that no one since Him has healed like that. So it is no good our talking of a theoretical faith which we ourselves cannot operate.

But more than that. Paul did not write of total healing for the body; and can anyone have greater faith than Paul who did raise the dead, and spoke of 'mighty signs and wonders by the power of the Spirit of God'? But Paul qualified his great victory chapter, Romans 8, by saying that we 'groan within ourselves, waiting for the adoption, to wit, the redemption of our body'. He spoke of the body dead because of sin, and that it will be quickened, but the future, not present tense is used. 'The outward man perishes', he said, and advised his own chosen successor, Timothy, not to get healing, but 'to take a little wine for thy stomach's sake and thine often infirmities'. He said the same of his companion Trophimus whom he had 'left at Miletum sick'; and all this quite apart from the controversial question of what his own unhealed 'thorn in the flesh' was, though most of us think it was blindness.

Where do we stand then between possible healing and continued sickness? I think it fits right in to our whole position – that we are not body people, but spirit people. We are spirits inhabiting temporary tabernacles. But, as with all things material, we have had our minds set more on the physical than the spiritual. We are too body-minded instead of being Spirit-minded. At a meeting which is opened for requests for prayer, almost always two-thirds of them centre round the body.

But suppose we apply our same principle of matter or Spirit believing to our bodies. We say that what we are believing in is real to us and we are contributing to its reality. Well, while we believe in our body condition, is that not what many say today, including many in the medical profession – that a lot of our ill-health is the product of our minds, our believing in sickness? The world psychosomatic is an in-word for today. Now refer that to my immediate 'sick' condition. I am hurting, so I am surely tempted to believe that my sickness is the reality. So it is on the physical level. But now, as in all these other ways, we have talked about, we transfer our believing to who we really are, human spirits in union with the Divine Spirit, and consequently perfect in Him and in His perfect life. We simply are in the perfection of eternal life, for 'by one offering He hath perfected for ever them that are sanctified'; and to this fact we attach our believing, and not to our body condition; and say so with the expressed word of faith. We *are* in perfect health *in Him*, or we should rather say in perfect life in Him, for health and sickness are part of that divided outlook through the Fall. This is the essential. This is the victory – to see ourselves perfect in Him, and say so with praise, when our bodily condition is obviously imperfect. This means reality to us is spirit, our human spirits in His Spirit. We have our sick physical condition, and it is having its obvious effects on us and we are taking any available remedies for it; but we keep maintaining that that is not who we really are or where we really are. We really are in life 'in Him'.

This also means that we are accepting for the present moment that we have a bodily condition of sickness, and that this is His present deliberate will for us. He 'determined' this for us. He 'gave' us this messenger of Satan to buffet us, if we use Paul's word. So we praise Him for it, as well as in it. It is when we do that, we can settle our believings in Him instead of our bodies. That is a dying in Christ to flesh-believing and a rising to Spirit-believing.

When we are clear in this, by the evidence of being able to praise the Lord, then the secondary word of faith is possible. We can say that God heals the body now. We can speak the word of healing now for our physical condition, or fellow-believers can lay hands on us, or anoint us according to the Scriptures. And let us speak that word without compromise. 'I will. Be thou healed.'

Now when Jesus spoke such words of faith, the healings were immediate, and sometimes with the apostles, and there are many present-day instances of immediate healing. But not so in thousands of others of us. This is where we need to be careful not to be trapped into going back on our word of faith. Is it because of lack of faith? Well, that can be said of all of us, for none on earth manifest the faith of Jesus who healed all. We must all face up to Paul's warning to 'think soberly, according as God hath dealt to every man the measure of faith'. Therefore if there is not an immediate healing, beware of accepting false condemnation, especially when others say, 'Why haven't you faith?', or if others are healed at a healing meeting and you are not. If I have spoken that word of faith that I am healed, and apparently I am not, then I can so easily swing back to that old negative believing which looks at my body and judges by outer sight. Then down I go again in the bonds of the visible and unbelief. But I am to learn to accept God's time-table, and that once my faith is fixed, my faith is fixed. I do not look down to see how and where the answer comes. The word of healing has been spoken, and I walk on in the spirit, not body-minded, but Spirit-minded, and people catch that from us. And in that present condition Christ is magnified in our body 'whether by life or by death'. When we are praising and thanking God, yet still in physical ill-health, we are doing something the world cannot do, and demonstrating a power not of ourselves.

Incidentally, that is why we do not help people in their illness by sympathy which keeps attention on their suffering condition. We truly help by the much more costly compassion, rather than sympathy, which loves people enough to help them to praise the Lord in their condition, even though by saying that to some who are feeding on their own self-pity, we may get a sharp comeback. But that is compassion – loving people by doing what I know is best for them, and not by what is easiest and most comfortable for me in commiserating with them.

Then where is the healing or deliverance? It often does come, sometimes suddenly and miraculously. It may come gradually and sometimes it may never come in the body. But one thing is certain, we shall know and see that God has done what we said He would do. We shall be able to say, 'Yes, that's why I had this suffering. Look, this was God's full answer, I would not have had any other.' That will take us right up to the topmost point Paul reached, when God made it plain to him that his 'thorn' would never be removed in the way he first requested. But he received so much more from God, which he has been able to pass on by his witness to countless millions, and which he could have passed on in no other way, when God said, 'My grace is sufficient for thee; for my strength is made perfect in weakness'; and that took him another big stride forward when he said, 'I now welcome all kinds of physical or human frustrations, because I've discovered that it is when I am weak that I am strong.' He got the total answer to his prayer of faith for healing; and so do I, somewhere along the line. Stick to the word, 'The just shall live by faith: but if any man draw back, my soul shall have no pleasure in him.'

But one balancing word should be added. Don't let's

be fools. There is in fact not a single completely perfect body on earth. All have some physical disabilities. We thank God for every gift of healing and bless those called to minister that way in the Body of Christ. May they not be moved from using their gift to the full. Praise God for those who do get healed in great public 'healing' meetings, or privately. Praise God for the many who find Christ as Saviour when they came to the meetings for body healing. But for a great many of us, our healing is the flow of the life of God in our mortal bodies, while we continue with some disabilities; but we go on and on despite them. My wife, Pauline, has never been robust and has suffered much physically, but on she goes, now nearing eighty, and thanking God for what she has learned of Him through suffering. I had a damaged knee through football when young, and then was shot in the same leg in World War I, and had knee surgery twice, and walk with a leg somewhat out of the straight till today. For this I was given a small disability pension. But I started out in the Congo (Zaire) over fifty years ago, when we had to walk the forest tracks to the villages. My knee sometimes caused trouble with sinovitis or tempoary dislocation, but not really disabling. I foolishly (?) resigned the pension as not really needing it! Five years ago I was told the knee is full of arthritis, and if I had trouble, the only thing would be to stiffen the leg. But there is no trouble, and I still keep on the move in tours of meetings. It had been the quickening life of God overflowing an unhealed condition, and that is all I have needed. That is a trivial illustration compared to so many, but the principle is the same. In perfect life in Christ, yes now and forever. In physical healing, maybe; sometimes sudden, sometimes gradual, sometimes not at all, but praising God anyhow and continuing in His overflow of life: and sometimes best of all, out of this mortal body and with Christ which is far better: and adieu till we meet again for ever!

Chapter Twenty-six

We Have Reached the Top

We now reach the summit. We said from the beginning that no greater statement was ever made than that God is love, because that reveals the heartbeat of the universe, when we know what kind of person He is who is the All in All of the universe: 'of Whom and through Whom and to Whom are all things', and 'by Whom all things consists', and who 'gathers together in one all things in Christ', having by Him 'reconciled all things to Himself'. And we therefore know that, being love, He is for others; and that is all He is, because that is all love is; and that that is why in the last book of the Bible, we have constantly revealed to us that He is 'The Lamb on the throne'. And we saw that if He had appointed His Son heir of all things, and through His Son brought us, the many sons, to glory as His brethren and co-heirs, then we are co-inheritors of the universe; and we can only safely own, manage and develop His universe, if we have that same spontaneous love-nature that He has. That is precisely the meaning and purpose of the long long trail of human history, and His own total identification with us on that trail. He descending to our hell for us, so that we now ascend to His heaven with Him; and the outcome of our identification with Him on this descent-ascent, is that we now partake of His divine nature, and that nature is love. In union with Him, we are lambs and other-lovers, because in the mystery of Spirit-unity, we are He who is love in our human forms, the Father in the sons by the Spirit.

So here is our summit, the third and final grade in the ascent, through cross to resurrection to ascension, as Paul reveals to us in his ascension letter to the Ephesians. Just as He puts those stages of ascent into practical terms in his Roman letter, in our justification in Christ's death (Chapters 3–5), union with Him in His resurrection (Chapters 6–8), and co-saviourhood with him in His ascension (Chapters 9–15); or as John so succinctly put it, by comparison with the stages in nature by which an infant reaches manhood: 'I write unto you, little children ... young men ... fathers. Infants who start life in total dependence on their parents ('Your sins are forgiven you for His name's sake, and you know the Father'): adolescents who have to discover their own inner resources to be adequate for life ('you are strong, and the word of God abides in you, and you have overcome the wicked one'): and then – what we are now talking about – this third grade of adults, about whom he makes this curious statement, 'because ye have known Him that is from the beginning': not here called the Father in the personal relationship sense, but the One, beyond any names, who is 'from everlasting to everlasting' in His love-activities, and we now identified with Him.

That means this third revolutionary fact about us, and its vast implications. As sons in His universe, we are as He is; and if His total being is for others, so is ours. But that is not the usual way we look at our lives. We think rather of the effect of things on ourselves. 'Why has this happened to me? Why do I seem on the shelf? Why do others have it easier? Am I reaping the harvest of my own mistakes? I wish He would let up on me a little. And so on. But now we begin to practise the third recognition: the first, that I am His and He mine: the second, that it is He living my life: the third that as He is for others, so am I – and nothing else.

I say practise recognizing this, because we are already in this threefold relationship with Him. He did it, not we. We don't attain, we just find ourselves to be what we are in Him. It was He who died, He who arose, and He who ascended; and marvellously, these are just what we now are. We are dead with Him, risen with Him, ascended with Him. And being now 'seated with Him in the heavenlies' by no means being a do-nothing. When a man sits down in the evening to his dinner after his day's work, that is not the end of his day's activities. He just sits down thankful that that day's job is finished; but now, let's get on with the evening's activities! So when Jesus 'sat down at the right hand of the Majesty on high', that was only the beginning of a new form of activity. As He had now completed our salvation, so now He goes forth by His Spirit in His ascended body 'to lead captivity captive and give gifts unto men', to change the devil's slaves into His love-slaves, and to endow us with the gift to be His body-builders in the world.

Now the danger arises of us thinking that we must rush about being not for ourselves, but for others. By no means. Just go on being yourself and don't give a thought about being for others. Just run your own life, Accept yourself, be yourself, love yourself! Appreciate

143

that you are a special person, specially gifted by God. For what? That's not your business. Don't try and run His business! Get on with your daily occupations and putting all your heart into them. But of course, there's a catch in that. You are not really yourself, but Christ in you, Christ the real you. And He is for others, and He knows exactly how He will reach others by you in your special life's situation and with your special equipment, of which you may not be even conscious, and probably good that you are not! If you try to fuss around being something for others, for your neighbours, for good works in your church, your town or out to the world, you may just be so occupied in the wrong direction that He will have to do some more work on you to get you where He really wants you!

He is love in us, other-love, so you just can't help yourself. Without any kind of human effort, you just find yourself drawn into maybe love-contacts with naturally unpleasant neighbours; you find folks somehow get in touch with you, because you are free from fussing about your own affairs or theirs, just free to love, not to condemn or judge or try to change them, and one or another will be coming to you and pouring out their burdens. Or you will be invited to join this or that group where you meet people, or take this class for teaching, or represent this society which is taking the gospel to the world, or who knows what? But when folks do begin to find you are available, you have to beware against being back 'under law'; and this especially if you are a member of an active local church and therefore because you are a member, you must and ought to attend this or that, or participate in this or that. No, you are not first a member of a local church. You are first a member of the world body of

144

Christ, and He is your Heavenly Pastor who alone can order you here or there; so if He is loving others by you, then you must die to being just the active church-member who had the approbation of your church fellowship! The Spirit is original in each of us, and He will get His original plan into action by you in some way which frees you from man-pleasing: and a pastor through whom God is going to do His real work must equally die to what his people think he ought to be, and still more dangerously what his denomination can approve, if he is called to be a denominational man; and God does call many to be stay-inners as well as those called to be 'come-outers'. But promotion in the Holy Spirit and with His mighty enduement comes not from east or west or from the human hierarchy, but from God; and only death leads to life.

So we are back on the usual paradox – do nothing which stems from self-effort. But in being a do-nothing, you will actually be a do-everything, because the Real Doer whose aim is to get the world back to Himself will surely be busy by you in His own way and time. Yet watch even there when we say He will be busy by you, because times will come when you will appear to be useless on the shelf, as if God has forgotten you (how crazy can we be!), and the only word left which can suit you is, 'Be still, and know that I am God'. Very well then, be still; and if God wants to be lazy in you, let Him be!

But get it again, there is no other meaning to life for eternity than that we are for others, because that is all God is. *That* at least is the whole meaning of being a person – a person for others. And the plain proof in ourselves is that when we can be some help to others, the bells always ring within us. Precisely! We are in tune with the Infinite, and therefore the inner music is harmony. Even a child finds a secret satisfaction when he does share something with his little brother, especially if it is something he valued. Those bells are ringing!

So, first, we have to get accustomed to practising this recognition; and that means when things are hurting in life and we by our normal human reactions don't like it and are inclined to ask, 'Why has that happened to me?' then we practise the habit, the same as ever, of transferring our believings from what appears a hurtful condition to me, and replacing it with the recognition that it had only one purpose – something for others. Somewhere by this hurtful thing, Christ is going to reveal Himself to others by us, maybe as a start just by our praising, accepting attitude in place of the usual moaning and kicking.

Chapter Twenty-seven

Come Now . . . You

There is one further and final place. Just as everything that happens to me is geared now for others, and I practise accepting that as a permanent fact; so there are special areas of my life when I fully recognize that I am for others, for some special others, and I accept that. This is what the Bible speaks of as the intercession of a royal priest – the highest position given us on earth. And every one of us is a priest and intercessor. We only have to discover that and learn its meaning.

A priest, the Bible says, in Hebrews 5:1, is an ordinary human, you and I, 'taken from among men', in other words, out of this world into Christ by the new birth. Then he is 'ordained for men', in other words, is conscious of some special commission relating to some special people. Then he is 'ordained for men in things pertaining to God', in other words, to be responsible for bringing them to Christ. So a priest is not some special type of person whom unfortunately we wrongly call 'Reverend', and who equally unfortunately presents himself as different from the rest of us by special clothing, vestments or what ever; (though the Holy Spirit does greatly use many who do have special religious garb and titles, because He uses all of us,

147

though we all have some human quirks or other!). But we have to rescue the Biblical meaning of a priest from these connotations which the organized church have wrongly given to the office. We are all priests, because we all have commissions for others. We are royal priests because we have our authority from the Ascended Christ, and so function authoritatively in His name.

But to be a priest is to be an intercessor. That is the height of his calling: and an intercessor takes the place of those he intercedes for, and is responsible to bring them to God. That is something different from the exercise of prayer and faith in general. It means that there are defined boundaries to this special commission. I am conscious that this person, this particular set of people, this class, this church fellowship, this mission field, this special group I am called to minister to, this has been set apart for me. Now that again I don't seek out. It seeks me out. I mean that as my heart and eyes are open to where the Lord placed me, and I find myself caught up or involved with certain people or special interests, it will dawn on me that God has put me just there; obviously I am involved with them, and I can sense a direct word from the Lord, 'That is for you. I have put you there, I have stirred your heart with special interest in them, now go to it. You are My intercessor for them.' So there are special commissions. I have clearly seen and accepted this in each stage of my life. Perhaps it has not occurred to you to look at yourself that way. You are a royal priest. You are an intercessor. For what particularly?

An intercessor is a person, God's man, who stands in the gap, that is how the Bible puts it. Just you for that gap. Lots of general needs, lot of general interests, but this is particular – *for you*. And what does that mean for you? Plenty. It is your highest privilege on earth. This is now you for others in reality. An intercessor has no strings attached. As far as he is able, he takes the place of the one he intercedes for. It is said of the Saviour that He poured out His soul unto death, and so made intercession for the transgressors. Vicarious is the word. He took our place that we might take His place. He went to the limit to fulfil this, and so by the law of harvest, the fruit had to appear – for He Himself said, if a corn of wheat dies, it brings forth much fruit.

So for us it does not mean some passing prayer and faith interest in which we can passingly take a share. It means that this intercession is specifically mine to see through, and there is no giving up on it. I will pay the price, and the fruit must follow. There is no may about it, only a must. In my army days I had to be a witness in my regiment – to officers and soldiers alike. In my college days I had to win fellow-students to Christ, and I did, and that was when God gave us the start of the Inter Varsity Christian Fellowship. In my calling to a place of responsibility as secretary in our Worldwide Evangelization Crusade, I had to see new fields entered with the gospel; and when the Lord first gave me that 'had to' we were just two of us and now about 1,200. These days I know I 'have to' keep going around sharing the kind of things I am now writing about. Always a 'have to', with a no-limit price-tag attached. And it can also include my intercession for single souls who 'have to' find Christ, and I'm not letting go on that.

Then it goes farther – into the physical and material. At this point we have no hold-backs. God is saying, I have come to do so and so, and I have come to do it through you. On a praying level the thing may happen; on an interceding level it must. If we just pray for this or that, it may happen. If we accept an intercession, it must. For this our lives are on the altar. 'A body hast Thou prepared Me', Jesus said: and 'through the offering of the body of Jesus Christ we are sanctified'.

So intercession is not only the spoken word of faith, but the persistent giving of ourselves by whatever ways God indicates to see the fulfilment. It is Paul's filling up 'that which is behind of the afflictions of Christ in my flesh for His body's sake'. 'So death worketh in us, but life in you.' That is why I think one of the top-most sayings in the Bible is Isaiah's prophecy about Christ: 'It pleased the Lord to bruise Him.' The Father's greatest pleasure was when in His Son He had one upon whom He could put the full weight of bodily sacrifice for the whole world. It pleases the Lord if He can bruise us for those He has sent us to save, and we can take the bruises. There are no limits to that. I had the profound influence in my life of my own father-in-law, C. T. Studd, who had said to the Lord at the moment of his full consecration when England's greatest cricketer, 'If Jesus Christ, God's Son, gave his life to save me, I can only be an honest Christian if I give my life for Him.' And God took him at his word. Called from all his earthly glory as a cricketer to inland China: while there, giving away every penny of his large inheritance, probably worth a quarter of a million in today's values, for the spread of the gospel: living his last sixteen years in the heart of Africa in his bamboo home surrounded by the Africans he loved and came to win for Christ. When Pauline, my wife and his daughter, saw him for the last time while we sat by his simple African bed until 3.00

a.m., knowing we were not likely to see him on earth again, he said to her, 'Pauline, I should like to give you something before you go', then looking round the few boxes of necessities which were all he possessed, he said, 'But I gave it all to Jesus long ago'. And another time he had said, 'My only regret is that I had not more to sacrifice for Jesus.' And what a harvest! The thousands who have found Christ in the heart of Africa, and the hundreds of thousands who heard of Him and many come to know Him in forty different countries, through those who later joined this Worldwide Crusade he founded.

We don't follow or imitate a man, but we learn a great principle: God will privilege every one of us as intercessors to be poured out in some way in hours, in work, in witness, by money, by health, by sacrificial use of our homes, by sacrifice of loved ones, by our lives, and with no let-up in our readiness for any involvement while we have life and breath. Our glory is the cross, not only His cross, but that we may take up ours with Him, 'the cross of our Lord Jesus Christ by whom the world is crucified to me, and I unto the world'; and not just the cross which delivered me, but which I can share for the world's deliverance. What greater final word can there be than Paul's:

I count all things but loss for the excellency of the knowledge of Christ Jesus my Lord: for whom I have suffered the loss of all things, and do count them but dung, that I may win Christ . . . that I may know Him, and the power of His resurrection, and the fellowship of His sufferings, being made conformable to His death . . . Brethren I count not myself to have apprehended: but this one thing I do, forgetting those things that are behind, and reaching forth unto those things that are before, I press toward the mark for the prize of the high calling of God in Christ Jesus. (Philippians 3:8–14.)

Epilogue

A Love Story

Dick and Laurie Hills are dear friends of mine with whom I often stay in Alexandria, Virginia, a city across the Potomac from Washington. Dick is Assistant Superintendent of Schools and also much involved in the Young Life Movement. Laurie, who has brought up a family of three and also paints portraits, is a leader of several Fellowship and Bible groups in the neighbourhood. Laurie writes the following:

I met a man who looked at me. No, he looked into me. He knew, and I knew he knew that I had looked all my life for my real self, for fulfilment, and I was lost because I was out of looking places. His eyes were full of the kind of thing that melted my long since frozen soul. I even tentatively ventured to believe that this was actually the kind of thing people looked for when they said they were looking for love. When he finally spoke, I was eager for his words. He said, 'I know who you were meant to be. Only give your permission and I will make it so.' His eyes continued to hold mine like a vice. He had such drawing power and his proposal such promise, that every part of me wanted to shout, 'Yes!' Every part, that is, except the part of me that said, 'Don't kid yourself. It might work for someone else, this magic trick he has up his sleeve. But you know you well enough to know that you're a jinx!'

What was he doing to me with his eyes? He must know my thoughts, for as his gaze penetrated ever deeper into my relaxing soul, I felt the self-hatred trickling away. And I knew he didn't consider me a jinx. I said with a freedom surprising to me, 'Yes, yes, as soon as possible, but how can we manage this and how long will it take?' Nagged by memories of old and not-so-old failures, I was totally unprepared for his answer. 'It is done. The moment your heart assented, before you spoke a word, it was done. The emptiness of self has been replaced by my Life. I am the Source of Life. This is what you were always meant to be, a container for my Life.'

I was, of course, glad to know this, but I had expected a feeling of elation, or strength, or fulfilment. That's what I had expected – a feeling of fulfilment. Oh, there would be no escaping this Life, for he was reading my thoughts again. 'You are disappointed? You want a feeling as a sign that I'm here? My love, believe what I tell you. I have died and carried your empty self with me to that death so I could live my Life in you.' I believed and thought about what my Beloved had said was truth. When I found that I couldn't believe, I cried, 'I do believe, but help thou mine unbelief!' And that loved Life within gave peace.

Then one day the words He had told me to believe exploded into meaning. Things often happen that way these days, unplanned things. And I shouted, 'He did save me from myself and He did put his own Life in its place.' And I felt! I felt all the good emotions that I ever dreamed of feeling, and they were so strong that they demanded to be shared with friends who had tried to help me find who I was.

As the intimacy of this Good that had come began to grasp my consciousness. I said to my Beloved, 'I must try to make myself look and act better because you are living in me. I will try to find ways.' He was silent, and I was busy striving to improve the image I projected; for, after all, I was a Life carrier. My bearing must demonstrate my importance. I looked, I inquired, I tried, I tired. I experimented and I failed and wondered why He was so silent. He should he helping me. After all, this was to show him how much I appreciated what He had done for me.

I remember those as joyless days. I was so busy outside trying to create ways to make him proud that He had chosen to live in me and let others see my high estate that I had had no time for enjoying him, as I had in the beginning. Life was becoming almost as it was before. One day I came rushing home with great and high expectations. I went flying to him, waving a paper with ten rules beautifully lettered. These, I had been told by a religious-looking man, if kept, would please any good man. He saw them and said quietly. 'Will you keep them?' 'Yes!' said I, exhilarated at the thought of a good solid task to tackle. I memorized the rules first. They were simple. All that striving and here was the answer Why hadn't I run into that man before, and what did my Beloved mean, 'Would I keep them?' – just ten simple rules!! I had to skip the first one since it wasn't as solid as I had thought. I simply didn't know whether I had any other gods before him. Sometimes I couldn't be sure I wasn't my own god. I had similar problems with the others. Why was life becoming so complicated and unfulfilled again?

I went to him. 'I'm a failure. I promised I'd keep those ten rules; I can't keep one.'

His answer, 'No one ever has, except me. My Life being lived in you fulfils them all.'

Hurt and pouting, I said, 'Is there nothing I can do to please you?'

'Are you through trying, beloved?' he asked.

I sank down before him with a weary nod of assent. 'Then I'm pleased,' he said. As if he had kept me off balance long enough, he hastened to answer my quizzical look with, 'When my love for you prompted me to die for you, I took everything of you with me into death. When we resumed life again, the burden was gone. I have made you pleasing to me. You had to do nothing but want me – for me to live in you. Now I have waited for you to want me to live through you. Do you want me to?'

A trapped feeling began to grip me – almost a fear. Fear! Fear? In the face of such great love? What could I fear? Losing control? Maybe. Violation of my personhood? That's a laugh. I was no person before He came, and I knew He was no violator. Was my fear that this couldn't be for real? I blurted out, 'You mean to tell me there is *no* price-tag attached to anything you do for me? Life's not like that!!'

'Death,' came his cryptic answer.

My reeling thoughts scurried after the meaning. There it was! His was a life I couldn't understand, because the life I had thought was life, was death. Staggering!! Out of this world!! Could I stand it, this Life?

No more striving to be something, because Another was already everything in me, for me, through me? My competitive soul already suffered at this prospect.

I thought he must soon become impatient. He had asked that question so long ago and I had not answered. I looked and he seemed to have eternity to wait. But I didn't. 'One more question. If I chose, could I now or ever escape your fearful love?'

'You are sealed,' he said with finality.

'But if I can't do anything!'

'Ah, my love, you are my Life in the world. You may come begging for less action; and *do*? Have you forgotten the time you first knew I loved you? I did tell you *one* thing, but you found you needed me even to do that.'

Ruefully I thought, 'How could I forget that struggle? It was a hard thing to *believe* when you wanted a feeling.' Believe – yeah! It figures! A love that has done everything for me so he can be everything through me leaves nothing but to believe this preposterous presumptuous truth.

And then as if to mockingly tease a little, he said, 'And the most presumptuous thing of all you may not believe for a little while. I'm preparing you to rule the universe with me through all eternity. Are you ready? Can you take the preparation?' And then I remembered the night I asked Him who He was. He had said, 'I Am'. I fell asleep waiting for Him to finish the sentence; but He *had* finished the sentence, hadn't He?!! He is the only Person there is!

'Ready? Oh, my God, you have made me ready. Take the preparation? You will take it in me. Who or what is there beside thee?'